YORK NOTES

MEASURE
FOR
MEASURE

WILLIAM SHAKESPEARE

NOTES BY EMMA SMITH

 Longman

York Press

Exterior picture of the Globe Theatre reproduced by permission of the
Raymond Mander and Joe Mitchenson Theatre Collection
Reconstruction of the Globe Theatre interior reprinted from Hodges;
'The Globe Restored' (1968) by permission of Oxford University Press

YORK PRESS
322 Old Brompton Road, London SW5 9JH

PEARSON EDUCATION LIMITED
Edinburgh Gate, Harlow,
Essex CM20 2JE, United Kingdom
Associated companies, branches and representatives throughout the world

First published 1999
This new and fully revised edition first published 2003
Sixth impression 2008

ISBN: 978-0-582-78430-7

Designed by Michelle Cannatella
Typeset by Land & Unwin (Data Sciences), Bugbrooke, Northamptonshire
Produced by Pearson Education Asia Limited, Hong Kong

CONTENTS

PART FOUR
CRITICAL HISTORY

PART FIVE
BACKGROUND

PART ONE

INTRODUCTION

HOW TO STUDY A PLAY

Studying on your own requires self-discipline and a carefully thought-out work plan in order to be effective.

- Drama is a special kind of writing (the technical term is 'genre') because it needs a performance in the theatre to arrive at a full interpretation of its meaning. Try to imagine that you are a member of the audience when reading the play. Think about how it could be presented on the stage, not just about the words on the page.

- Drama is always about conflict of some sort (which may be below the surface). Identify the conflicts in the play and you will be close to identifying the large ideas or themes which bind all the parts together.

- Make careful notes on themes, character, plot and any sub-plots of the play.

- Why do you like or dislike the characters in the play? How do your feelings towards them develop and change?

- Playwrights find non-realistic ways of allowing an audience to see into the minds and motives of their characters, for example, **soliloquy**, **aside** or music. Consider how such dramatic devices are used in the play you are studying.

- Think of the playwright writing the play. Why were these particular arrangements of events, characters and speeches chosen?

- Cite exact sources for all quotations, whether from the text itself or from critical commentaries. Wherever possible find your own examples from the play to back up your opinions.

- Where appropriate, comment in detail on the language of the passage you have quoted.

- Always express your ideas in your own words.

These York Notes offer an introduction to *Measure for Measure* and cannot substitute for close reading of the text and the study of secondary sources.

? QUESTION

How many conflicts can you identify in *Measure for Measure*?

READING *MEASURE FOR MEASURE*

CHECK THE FILM

The 1994 BBC production of the play set it amid the bars, brothels and sex shops of a seedy, modern metropolis.

Is it right to sleep with someone in return for a favour? Is a woman's virginity worth more than a man's life? Should prostitution be punished? Are those in power who preach about sexual morality hypocrites? Should society punish a man for getting his girlfriend pregnant? Is there a place for mercy in the legal system? Should we be interested in the private morality of public figures? Can the punishment ever fit the crime? Put like this, the questions asked by *Measure for Measure* are revealed to be strikingly modern: no wonder recent productions have dressed Angelo in a pinstripe suit and peopled Shakespeare's Vienna with the petty criminals and prostitutes of a modern-day urban underworld. In this play, Shakespeare puts morality and the law itself on trial, but the verdict can only be delivered by the audience. Of all Shakespeare's plays, it is the one which is most insistently full of questions, and which most clearly represents the grey areas which make up individual and social morality, now as well as in seventeenth-century England. Shakespeare's picture of urban life is darkly comic, as the play explores the intersections between different moral codes and standards while refusing ultimately to endorse any single viewpoint over another. The more you read or watch the play the more complicated and the more rewarding its ambiguities become.

Measure for Measure, then, is heavy on questions and correspondingly light on answers. Its characters and their actions and belief systems can be interpreted in more than one way: like those optical illusions that show a picture which, viewed one way is a rabbit and another a duck, it all depends how you look. Is Isabella heartless and selfish, or is she steadfastly true to a higher calling? Are the Duke's motives benevolent or sinister? Is Angelo a good man who is tempted or a hypocrite who preaches abstinence while craving indulgence? Do the play's final marriages symbolise social harmony or authoritarian control? Many of these choices, and others like them, become clearer through performance, and these Notes will refer to the play in the theatre wherever this offers a useful perspective. *Measure for Measure*'s predominant mode is one of questioning – we might call it interrogative – a play which forces us to think about the issues it presents and to supplement it with our own moral code. It is rather like a theatrical version of the game 'Scruples', in which players are confronted with a moral dilemma and must defend their own judgement to the others.

When Shakespeare's works were first gathered together for publication in the First Folio text of 1623, *Measure for Measure* was included among the comedies. Many readers have found this generic attribution inappropriate to this dark and complex play, preferring to see comedies as lightweight and frothy, concerned with love and romance rather than commercial sex and judicial punishment. At the end of the nineteenth century, the critic F.S. Boas dubbed *Measure for Measure*, along with *All's Well that Ends Well*, *Troilus and Cressida* and *Hamlet*, as a 'problem play', meaning that all four plays have as their core a moral or philosophical problem which the action is trying to resolve. But however useful it may be to highlight the problem of *Measure for Measure* – although it might be more difficult to isolate just a single problem – it is important not to forget its close fit with many of the features of Shakespearean comedy. The Jacobean playwright Thomas Heywood gives a contemporary view of a simple difference between comedy and tragedy: 'comedies begin in trouble and end in peace; tragedies begin in calms and end in tempest'. *Measure for Measure* certainly begins 'in trouble' – the Duke's abdication – but it is less clear that its conclusion, stage-managed by the Duke, represents the restoration of peace. Comedies feature the courtship of pairs of lovers, ending with their marriage, typically, sex itself is sublimated into the language of wooing, and we leave the main characters, as it were, at the bedroom door. In ending with marriages, *Measure for Measure* fulfils one of the common features of Shakespearean comedy as exemplified in *As You Like It* or *A Midsummer Night's Dream*, but in allowing, even depending on sex before marriage, *Measure for Measure* has disrupted the usual order of events. Even its marriages raise more questions than they offer solutions. Can Angelo and Mariana be happy, given the betrayal and deception which has engineered their union? Does Isabella, who is deafeningly silent in response to the Duke's proposal, accept her sudden lover, and if so, why doesn't she speak?

> **CONTEXT**
>
> The First Folio is the first collected edition of Shakespeare's plays, published posthumously in 1623. The word 'folio' refers to the large size of the book made from sheets of paper with only one fold.

QUESTION

Until the second half of the twentieth century, *Measure for Measure* was not a popular play for readers or audiences. What do you think are the reasons?

The fact that Shakespeare's plays are still studied and performed today may encourage us to think of them as timeless or perennial, rather than as specific to the culture and historical period of their composition. Looking at their immediate context can, however, offer insights into their concerns and interests. *Measure for Measure* was first performed at the court of the new King of England, James I, in 1604. The play is set in a city rife with problems of public morality – much like the way in which many contemporaries saw their own city, London. There are parallels between Shakespeare's Vienna and the London of the early seventeenth century, and, for the play's first audiences, who were extremely clued in to topical references in the drama, there may be covert parallels between the Duke and James himself. It is this combination of sex, politics and the law which gives the play its tabloid *frisson* and its insistent moral equivocation, and which makes studying *Measure for Measure* so engaging and rewarding.

PART TWO

THE TEXT

NOTE ON THE TEXT

On 26 December 1604, a play called 'Mesur for Mesur', written by 'Shaxberd' (in an age which had no standardised spelling, even proper names are written erratically, and even by their owners) was performed in the banqueting hall of the Palace of Whitehall in London. It is generally thought that the play was written earlier that same year, and that it may have been performed during the summer of 1604 in the public theatre. Some scholars have seen in Lucio's reference to the duke's 'composition with the King of Hungary' and the reply about 'peace' (I.2.1–4) an allusion to the peace negotiations between England and Spain which were taking place during the spring and summer of 1604, resulting in a peace declaration between the English sovereign and those of Spain and Austria in August. Another contemporary allusion may be uncovered in Pompey's announcement of a 'proclamation': 'All houses [brothels] in the suburbs of Vienna must be plucked down' (I.2.94–6).

The play was first published in 1623, eight years after Shakespeare's (or Shaxberd's) death, in the First Folio edition of 'Mr William Shakespeares Comedies Tragedies & Histories'. It was listed under 'comedies' on the contents page, and its title is given with added punctuation as *Measure, for measure*. All modern editions, therefore, including J. M. Nosworthy's New Penguin Shakespeare edition to which these Notes will refer, take this text as their basis. *Measure for Measure* is unusual in having a list of *dramatis personae* – 'The names of all the Actors' – and clearly defined location – 'The Scene Vienna' – appended to it in print. It is from this list of characters that the name of the Duke – Vincentio – and other details such as the description of Lucio as 'a fantastic' (someone who dresses or behaves eccentrically) and Escalus as 'an ancient Lord' are derived (see **Background**, on **The texts of Shakespeare's plays**).

CONTEXT

In September 1603 a law was proclaimed in London which allowed for the demolition of houses in the suburbs – where most brothels were located – in an attempt to stop the spread of the plague, and this order was enforced during the following months.

SYNOPSIS

Measure for Measure is set in Vienna. The Duke Vincentio has decided to give up his authority and place it temporarily in the hands of his deputy, Angelo. Angelo is charged with bringing lapsed laws back into force and tackling the city's problems of prostitution and sex outside marriage. Instead of leaving Vienna as he claims, however, the Duke remains, disguised as a friar, to observe matters during his supposed absence.

One of the first acts of the new regime is the arrest of Claudio, whose girlfriend Juliet is pregnant. Claudio is condemned to death, despite his defence that the couple had a marital contract and were only waiting on certain practicalities to have an official ceremony. Claudio asks his friend Lucio to inform Isabella, his sister, who is about to enter a convent. Isabella goes to Angelo to plead for her brother's life, and the austere deputy finds himself sexually attracted to her. At their second meeting he offers to spare Claudio if she agrees to have sex with him. Isabella is horrified, refuses, and goes to tell her brother. In this interview, Claudio attempts to persuade her to go along with Angelo's proposal, voicing his own fear of death. Isabella refuses. The disguised Duke tells Claudio to prepare himself for death, and tells Isabella of a way to resolve the situation. Angelo's jilted sweetheart, Mariana, will go in place of Isabella to the assignation so that, having consummated their relationship, Angelo will be forced into marrying her. The pair go to Mariana, she agrees to this plan, and meets her former fiancé under cover of darkness.

The next day Angelo orders that Claudio be executed. The Duke arranges that another prisoner be executed instead of Claudio, but Barnadine refuses to be hanged, so the head of Ragozine, a prisoner who has died, is substituted. Isabella is told by the Duke that Claudio is dead. The Duke makes preparations for his return to office, and arranges a public meeting with his deputy. Isabella accuses Angelo, Mariana claims him as her lawful husband, and the Duke reveals that he has been privy to Angelo's deeds during his supposed absence. The Duke threatens to execute Angelo as recompense for his execution of Claudio, but Mariana persuades Isabella to plead for her husband. Claudio is revealed to be alive, and the Duke proposes marriage to Isabella.

ACT I

SCENE 1

- Duke Vincentio expresses his intention to leave Vienna for a time and to appoint a deputy to take his place.
- The Duke invests his authority in Angelo, with Escalus as his second-in-command, and makes his departure.

The play opens with the Duke addressing one of his lords, Escalus, and noting his familiarity with the laws and governance of Vienna. The Duke sends for Angelo, telling Escalus that he has chosen Angelo to serve as deputy during his absence. He asks Escalus's opinion of this choice, and Escalus agrees that 'if any in Vienna be of worth / To undergo such ample grace and honour / It is Lord Angelo' (lines 22–4). Angelo enters and the Duke bestows on him his authority, appointing Escalus as his 'secondary' (line 46). Angelo protests that some test of his worth should be made before giving him such responsibility, but the Duke assures him of his choice. The Duke seems in a hurry to depart and wants to slip away without a public fuss. He tells Angelo that his powers in government are exactly those of the Duke himself, promises to write to them about his news, and leaves. There is no information about where, or why, he is going. Escalus asks Angelo about his role in the new order, and Angelo promises to discuss it with him.

COMMENTARY

The scene raises many questions. Why is the Duke so eager to leave? Where is he going? How long does he intend to be away? Why has he chosen Angelo to be his deputy? Why did he not choose Escalus, after describing him as knowledgeable and

CHECK THE BOOK

Frank Kermode's chapter on *Measure for Measure* in his book *Shakespeare's Language* (2000) discusses how this opening scene establishes a number of the linguistic motifs of the play.

CONTEXT

The 1996 RSC production of the play began with the Duke already gone – his words were disembodied and spoken as a recorded message left for his subordinates.

experienced in matters of government? In performance Escalus has sometimes been shown anticipating that he will be appointed during the Duke's speech up to about line 15, when the truth of his plans begins to dawn. Is the Duke, as some critics of the play have claimed, setting a test for Angelo? Does he already have suspicions of him? We are introduced to two of the major players in the drama, the Duke and Angelo. The Duke's purposes and motives seem mysterious here. His language is often oblique and its **syntax** knotted: take his first lines 'Of government the properties to unfold / Would seem in me t'affect speech and discourse' (lines 3–4) which is a contorted way of beginning to say that he does not need to tell Escalus about the properties of government. Perhaps this is a sign of psychological or emotional stress (see **Characterisation**). He expresses a desire for seclusion and a retreat from public life in his admission 'I love the people / But do not like to stage me to their eyes' (lines 67–8).

Angelo speaks only five times. He expresses himself the loyal servant of the Duke attending him in prompt answer to his summons; he asks for some further test of his mettle before the bestowal of such a duty; he offers to make some ceremony of the Duke's journey; he wishes blessings on his ruler's absence; and he promises to discuss Escalus's position with him. There are few clues to his character here. He does not question the Duke's decision except to offer his unworthiness, nor does he express surprise, pleasure, apprehension, humility, or any other emotion on hearing of this great change in his position. Loyalty, piety, and above all self-restraint, seem the keynotes of his responses.

GLOSSARY	
4	**lists** bounds
11	**pregnant** knowledgeable
14	**warp** deviate
17	**with special soul** with complete conviction
20	**organs** instruments
29	**belongings** abilities
30	**proper** exclusively

36–40	**Nature never … and use** Nature is like a creditor (one who is owed money) who never lends without stating how the loan should be used
41	**advertise** instruct
46	**secondary** deputy
48	**metal** (pun) metal/'mettle' – the imagery of stamping is from coin or medal minting
51	**leavened** considered
54	**prefers** presents
61	**something on** part of
70	**aves** commendations
78	**bottom of my place** basis of my duties

SCENE 2

- Evidence of the tone of Angelo's new regime is presented: all brothels are to be pulled down and Claudio is imprisoned awaiting execution for getting Juliet pregnant outside marriage.
- Claudio asks Lucio to contact his sister to get her to plead with Angelo for his life.

Lucio is engaged in some bawdy jesting with two gentlemen when they are joined by the brothel-keeper Mistress Overdone. They continue to joke about venereal diseases and their familiarity with her house until she tells them about Claudio, who is 'worth five thousand of you all' (lines 60–1) but who has been taken to prison. In three days he will be executed for getting Juliet pregnant. The men go off to investigate this rumour. Pompey, Mistress Overdone's servant, enters, as a gaoler and another hapless prisoner cross the stage. His offence, Pompey announces, is, like Claudio's: fornication. Pompey tells Mistress Overdone that there has been an order that all brothels are to be pulled down, and she fears for her livelihood. Pompey urges her to change her trade to innkeeper, and he will serve as her tapster. Claudio enters, under arrest, along with

CONTEXT

An Elizabethan lawyer writing in 1599 defined the kind of pre-contract apparently existing between Claudio and Juliet: 'although it be a degree under marriage, yet it is more than a determined purpose, yea more than a simple promise.'

Juliet. His gaoler tells him that he is acting on Angelo's authority. When Lucio asks Claudio what has happened, Claudio talks of excessive liberty which has brought about restraint. He tells Lucio that he and Juliet were betrothed and that she is his wife in all but name: 'She is fast my wife / Save that we do denunciation lack / Of outward order' (lines 146–8). They were waiting only for the settlement of her dowry before proceeding to a formal marriage ceremony. Claudio attributes his arrest to the zeal of the city's new ruler. Whereas before, under the Duke, the law was neglected for 'nineteen zodiacs' (line 167), now Angelo is treating the city as a rider on an unfamiliar horse who 'lets it straight feel the spur' (line 161) so as to establish his authority over the beast. Lucio suggests that they send after the Duke to seek his intervention in the case, but Claudio asserts that he is 'not to be found' (line 174). Instead he urges Lucio to find his sister, about to enter into a convent, and implore her to intercede with Angelo for mercy on his behalf. He expresses some confidence in her persuasive powers. Lucio promises to enact this commission.

COMMENTARY

The scene shifts from joking about prostitution and politics to their harsh realities as Angelo's new regime begins to bite. News of his plans to enforce laws more strictly reaches the community of reprobates who stand to lose by them. The speeches of Lucio, the gentlemen, Pompey and Mistress Overdone are all in prose, giving a freer, more earthy tone to the first part of the scene. This changes abruptly with the entrance of the captive Claudio at line 115. His **blank verse** speeches may signify his worth – Shakespeare often uses prose for lower-rank or comic characters – thereby distinguishing him from the other characters in the scene. This distinction is particularly obvious in the contrast between the speeches of Claudio and Lucio: where Claudio speaks the measured, educated and philosophical **iambic pentameters** of lines 124–9 or 144–54, Lucio responds in inappropriately chirpy and irreverent prose, making a joke of one who can 'speak so wisely under an arrest' (line 130) and offering the comfortless observation that 'thy head stands so tickle on thy shoulders' (line 171). His demeanour throughout the scene is jesting, even satirical. By contrast, Claudio is established as serious and sober, not the good-for-nothing we

CHECK THE BOOK

Russ McDonald's *Shakespeare and the Arts of Language* (2001) discusses Shakespeare's use of prose and verse, drawing on examples from across the plays.

might expect from the description of his crimes before his entrance. When he gives his side of the story, however, his assertion that he and Juliet were betrothed, having entered into a marriage contract, mitigates the severity of his actions and renders the authority's responses all the more extreme. His assessment of Angelo's actions as the new governor of Vienna is astute (lines 156–69). The theme of antithesis is established in his analysis of too much freedom leading to control: 'every scope by the immoderate use / Turns to restraint' (lines 126–7) (see **Themes**, on **Symmetry and antithesis; Freedom and restraint**)

CONTEXT

The motif of the disguised ruler was a popular theme in plays of the period, including John Marston's *The Malcontent* (1603), Thomas Middleton's *The Phoenix* (1604), and an episode in Act IV of Shakespeare's own *Henry V* (1599).

GLOSSARY

2	**composition** agreement
11	**razed** erased
22	**proportion** verse metre
29	**lists** selvages, edges of fabric such as velvet
32	**three-piled piece** expensive, triple-ply velvet
33	**piled** of fabric, but also punning on haemorrhoids and baldness as symptoms of syphilis
34	**French velvet** expensive imported fabric, but also punning on 'French' = venereal disease
43	**free** free from disease
49	**dolours** pains, with a pun on 'dollars', currency
51	**French crown** money, but punning on the baldness caused by syphilis
82	**sweat** sweating sickness, or Plague
83	**custom-shrunk** short of trade
92	**maid** small fish (with a pun on trouts, line 89)
95	**houses** bawdy houses, brothels
108	**tapster** barman
113	**provost** official who oversees executions
128	**ravin** devour
146	**She is fast my wife** they have pledged themselves by hand-fasting or betrothal
171	**an** if
	tickle precarious
177	**approbation** probation continued

CHECK THE FILM

In the 1978 BBC production, the bright, light setting of the convent where the nuns wear white, is a clear visual and moral contrast to the gloomy, half-lit streets of Vienna and its prison interiors.

182	prone apt
	dialect language of argument
189	tick-tack game involving knocking pegs into holes, hence an obvious sexual reference

SCENE 3

- The Duke meets Friar Thomas and explains the reasons for his retirement from office, citing the laxity into which the laws have fallen.
- There is need for a new authority to implement the laws' reinforcement.
- The Duke indicates his intention to remain in Vienna disguised as a friar.

The scene opens on a conversation between the Duke and a friar, and the Duke's first words seem to be denying that it is love which has caused him to abdicate his ducal responsibilities. The Duke tells the friar, whom he clearly knows well ('none knows better than you' – line 8) that he prefers a secluded life, and also that the laws of Vienna have fallen into disuse and are not respected. He has appointed Angelo, a 'man of stricture and firm abstinence' (line 12) in his place. The friar suggests that it would have been more imposing for the Duke himself to have applied the lapsed laws with more severity, but the Duke replies that, having presided over their decline, this new course would be a 'tyranny' (line 36). Rather he is going to entrust it to Angelo while remaining in Vienna in the guise of a friar to 'behold his sway' (line 43). He requests a habit and tuition in friar-like behaviour. The last lines of the scene seem to express some suspicion about how Angelo will bear his commission: 'Hence shall we see, / If power change purpose, what our seemers be.'

COMMENTARY

The main purpose of this scene is to add to our knowledge about the Duke. Friar Thomas's interjections serve only to prompt the Duke to tell us some of what we want to know and answer some of the questions aroused by the Duke's conduct in I.1. The Duke begins, however, in terms which seem designed to prolong the speculation about his actions and motives rather than end it. He has a 'purpose / More grave and wrinkled than the aims and ends / Of burning youth' (lines 4–6). In fact his 'purpose' seems more plural than singular: three justifications for his retirement from office are given in the scene, without any acknowledgement that this triplication makes his departure at once overdetermined (there are more reasons for an action than are strictly necessary) and yet still mysterious. The Duke even offers further reasons 'at our more leisure' (line 49). First the Duke reminds the friar, and the audience, of a character trait suggested in I.1.67–70, that of a personal desire for seclusion: 'I have ever loved the life removed' (line 8). Next, he discusses the way the law has fallen into disuse, echoing Claudio's analysis a few minutes earlier in lines 164–70 of the previous scene – although there is some disagreement over the length of this lapse, measured by Claudio at 'nineteen zodiacs' (I.2.167) and by the Duke at 'fourteen years' (line 21) (see **Treatment of time**). The friar's suggestion that the Duke himself would have had greater authority to 'unloose this tied-up justice' (line 32) also questions the logic of this factor as a legitimate reason for the Duke's withdrawal from rule. Thirdly, the Duke seems to have an ulterior motive, that of testing Angelo and observing whether his character is corrupted by power and whether he is truly as he seems. The fact that this last reason is emphatically placed at the end of the scene gives it added weight, and begins to flesh out earlier suggestions of a manipulative, even **Machiavellian**, side to his character (see **Extended commentaries, Text 1**).

CONTEXT

Machiavelli's *The Prince* (1513) contains one particular story which may be of relevance to *Measure for Measure*. It tells how the Duke Cesare Borgia took over a state in which the law had become disregarded, so he gave absolute powers to a deputy to reinstate good government. The deputy enforced the law cruelly and was unpopular with the people. Then Borgia returned and wanted to demonstrate that the repressive laws had come not from him but from the deputy. He arranged for the deputy's dissected body to be displayed in the central square. 'The ferocity of this scene,' writes Machiavelli, 'left the people at once stunned and satisfied.'

SCENE 4

- Isabella is discussing her imminent entry into the convent with one of the nuns.
- Isabella expresses her wish for stricter rules.
- Lucio arrives to tell her of her brother Claudio's imprisonment and of his wish that she should plead with Angelo on his behalf.
- Isabella agrees to try.

In conversation with the nun, Isabella asks about any 'farther privileges' (line 1) allowed to members of the order. The nun misunderstands and thinks she is keen for more freedom, whereas what Isabella wants is 'a more strict restraint' (line 4). This interchange is interrupted, however, by Lucio, who brings the news of Claudio's arrest. Isabella's response to the news that Juliet – whom she has known since their childhood – is pregnant is that the couple should marry. Lucio tells that this course of action is impossible under Angelo's government, describing his aversion to sensuality as an almost inhuman coldness, one whose blood is 'snow-broth' (line 58). He urges her to petition Angelo for a pardon for her brother. She is hesitant about her abilities, but is persuaded to try.

COMMENTARY

In giving us our first sight of Isabella, this scene completes Act I's series of introductions. From her first appearance on the stage, Isabella is associated with her religious vocation. She seems on the brink of joining the order when Lucio arrives, and throughout the rest of the play we never see her return to the convent. While her initial speech requests more restraint in the order of St Clare, her subsequent responses to Lucio's news show that she is not immune to worldly concerns. She is not shocked or judgemental about Juliet's pregnancy or her brother's culpability, but she is profoundly affected by the thought of Claudio's punishment. Her speeches become short, cropped lines expressive of her emotional response to the news. While she doubts her powers to affect Angelo, she resolves to do what she can, displaying a decisive practicality at odds with many stereotypical impressions of nuns. Lucio is

CONTEXT

Saint Clare was a religious order founded by St Clare and St Francis of Assisi in 1212 which imposed strict restrictions on its members who lived a life of poverty, charity and devotion.

eloquent in the scene, and through comparison with his previous appearance in I.2, it is possible to see his role as go-between emerging (see **Characterisation**). Also in comparison with I.2 it is noticeable that here he uses verse not prose, perhaps modulating his speech to the more austere atmosphere of the cloisters. His language is often unexpectedly poetic, as in his description on Isabella as 'a thing enskied and sainted' (line 34) and in the fruitful imagery of natural fertility used to describe Claudio and Juliet's relationship (lines 40–4). He also adds to the sense of mystery about the Duke in his remark that 'his givings-out [pronouncements] were of an infinite distance / From his true-meant design' (lines 54–5).

GLOSSARY		
17	stead	help
25	weary	long-winded
32	lapwing	in *Much Ado About Nothing* (III.1.24) Shakespeare seems to associate the lapwing with frivolous prattling
42	seedness	sown seeds
60	rebate	make dull
70	pith	purpose
86	Mother	prioress

ACT II

SCENE 1

- Escalus tries to suggest leniency towards Claudio but Angelo will hear none of it, and orders Claudio's execution for the next morning.
- Elbow the constable brings before them the garbled case of immorality against Pompey and Froth.
- Angelo impatiently leaves the matter to Escalus who dismisses them with a warning to reform.

CONTEXT

Like Angelo, the authorities in Shakespeare's London were keen to curb prostitution. An official sermon or homily described how 'above other vices, the outrageous seas of whoredom, fornication and uncleaness, have not only burst in, but also overflowed almost the whole world, unto the great dishonour of God, the exceeding infamy of the name of Christ, the notable decay of true Religion, and the utter destruction of the public wealth, and that so abundantly, that through the customable use thereof, this vice is grown into such an height, that in the manner among many, it is counted no sin at all, but rather a pastime, a dalliance, and but a touch of youth: not rebuked, but winked at: not punished, but laughed at.'

At the opening of the scene, Angelo and Escalus each talk about their view of the law. Angelo takes a hard line: the law must not be made a 'scarecrow' (line 1). Escalus tries to argue for Claudio as part of a good family, and suggests that even Angelo, 'most strait in virtue' (line 9), must recognise the force of temptation and therefore be merciful. Angelo admits the point about temptation but argues that the law is not discredited simply because those involved with it are not themselves perfect. Instead of pardoning the prisoner because his faults are so familiar, the judge who behaves likewise should himself be punished. Escalus does not argue further, and Angelo despatches the Provost with the warrant for Claudio's execution the next day. The austerity of this interchange is dispersed by the entry of Elbow the constable with two prisoners, Pompey and Froth. Elbow's unintelligible deposition uses many words wrongly (**malapropisms**) thus making a mockery of the scene. Pompey's speeches of self-defence are similarly digressive as he spins out Elbow's story and makes a counter-accusation about the character of Elbow's wife. Angelo gives up the courtroom in exasperation, and leaves Escalus in charge 'Hoping you'll find good cause to whip them all' (line 131). Escalus dismisses Froth and talks to Pompey, asking him about his business. Pompey's responses are irreverent but pragmatic, arguing that if prostitution is to be banned, then it will be necessary to 'geld and splay all the youth of the city' (lines 219–20). He is dismissed with a warning which he shows no signs of heeding. Escalus suggests that other local citizens might be found to take the burden of the office of constable from Elbow, and then invites the Justice, who has been silent since the beginning of the scene, home to dine with him. The Justice states simply that 'Lord Angelo is severe' (line 269), and Escalus makes an attempt to defend his superior's actions, but the scene ends with his mournful recognition that 'there is no remedy' for 'poor Claudio' (line 272).

CONTEXT
Shakespeare uses this humour derived from malapropisms elsewhere, particularly with the characters of Dogberry and Verges in his comedy *Much Ado About Nothing*.

COMMENTARY

It would be easy to see this scene as a long comic sequence sandwiched between two more serious and significant sections and to dismiss the buffoonery of Elbow and Pompey to focus on Escalus and Angelo. There is, however, more coherence in the themes, if not the tone, of the scene than this description suggests.

As often in Shakespeare's plays, comic characters revisit or rework themes and issues in the subplot to amplify their more 'serious' presentation elsewhere. Here in *Measure for Measure*, the central theme of the operation of justice and the law is considered on different levels and through different scenarios, as in this particular scene. The opening exchange between Escalus and Angelo offers an important insight into Angelo's behaviour. We have not seen him on stage since his few words in the first scene, although he has been mentioned in every intervening scene. His opening words 'we must not' establish his unbending fixity of opinion, and his mention of the 'terror' (line 4) shows how thoroughly he has assumed the role set out by the Duke, who uses the same word in I.1.19 and I.3.26. In using an image of animals to refer to the populace he could be seen to demonstrate a lack of human concern for the people. He is unaffected by Escalus's arguments for clemency, turning them round to support firmer punishments rather than leniency. He does, however, allow for the possibility of temptation, recognising that a member of the jury may be more guilty than the prisoner he is trying, or anyone would pick up and keep a jewel which if he had not seen he would not have been tempted by. His harshness, however, is represented as entirely consistent: he would wish for the same punishment on himself were he guilty as others. He asserts firmly, coldly, that 'he must die', and urges the Provost to arrange for Claudio to see his confessor before death. Escalus's speech beginning 'Well, heaven forgive him' (lines 37–40) has a curiously sententious, or moralising, tone which generalises from the particular situation. It is end-rhymed which may make it sound more proverbial, and it is not clear how it relates to the foregoing conversation. The irruption of Elbow and his prisoners into the scene introduces another tone, that of prose comedy. Elbow's confusion of words – 'benefactors' instead of 'malefactors', 'cardinally' for 'carnally' etc. – and Pompey's obfuscation give an ironic and comic twist to the earlier exchanges about justice and punishment. In place of the language of morality and desert invoked by Angelo and Escalus, Pompey presents his own, more practical and pragmatic code of behaviour as he summarises in his exit-line: 'I thank your worship for your good counsel; but I shall follow it as the flesh and fortune shall better determine' (lines 240–2). Pompey speaks the language of moral expediency in the knowledge that laws

CONTEXT

We don't know, of course, what Shakespeare thought of the legal profession, but one of the rebels in *2 Henry VI* memorably proposes 'the first thing we do, let's kill all the lawyers'.

do not change human behaviour nor cure human weakness. Amid all this side-tracking wordplay, the law looks like an ass in this scene: Angelo leaves in exasperation and the symbolically named figure of Justice is pointedly silent until the very last lines, when it is Angelo, not the 'benefactors', on whom he delivers a verdict (see **Themes**, on **Crime, punishment and justice**).

QUESTION

Examine the dramatic function of the play's comic scenes.

GLOSSARY	
5	**most strait** rigorous, strict
12–13	**Or that … purpose** if you could have acted decisively to have sex
19	**passing** passing sentence
23	**pregnant** obvious, full of meaning
30	**pattern out** be an example for
36	**pilgrimage** lifespan
39	**brakes** thickets
56	**comes off well** is well delivered
57	**quality** rank, status, or occupation
59	**out at elbow** (proverbial phrase) worn out, as of old clothes
61	**parcel** part-time
64	**hot-house** bath-house, but such places had a dubious reputation, hence a secondary meaning of brothel
66	**detest** Pompey's mistake for 'protest'
77	**cardinally** misused for 'carnally'
85	**misplaces** misuses words
87	**stewed prunes** commonly associated with prostitution and brothels
113	**Come me to** get to the point
122	**lower chair** unknown, but perhaps referring to an easy chair or couch
154	**an it like you** if it please you
	respected misused for 'suspected'
164	**Justice or Iniquity** ironic **personifications** attached to Elbow and Pompey, and which may refer to stock characters from medieval morality plays
166	**caitiff** villain
167	**Hannibal** misused for 'cannibal'

171	battery assault, but misused for 'slander' as Escalus observes
179	courses way of life
190	Overdone given the name of Overdone, but with a suggestion of sexual exhaustion
208	Pompey the Great Roman general defeated by Julius Caesar
219	geld and splay castrate and spay or sterilise
223	take order make arrangements
	drabs prostitutes
226	heading beheading
230	three pence a bay a ridiculously low rent, used by Pompey as a measure of unlikelihood
237	shrewd harsh
243	carman cart or wagon driver
258	go through with all perform all the duties
260	sufficient able
264	Eleven perhaps symbolic – the eleventh hour is just in time (see Matthew 20:1–16)

CONTEXT

Shakespeare deals with the original Pompey and Caesar more fully in his play *Julius Caesar* (c.1599).

SCENE 2

- Encouraged by Lucio, Isabella visits Angelo to plead for Claudio's life.
- Angelo will not yield and asserts the justice of his sentence.
- Angelo wavers and tells her to return the next day.
- Angelo reflects on how she has aroused his lust.

The scene begins with an exchange between Angelo and the Provost, in which the order of execution on Claudio is reiterated. The Provost tries to suggest that Angelo may repent of this command when it is too late but Angelo is unbending and threatens to appoint a new provost if he is not obeyed. Angelo also arranges for Juliet, 'the fornicatress', to be given 'needful, but not lavish, means' (lines 23–4). Isabella and Lucio are admitted. Isabella begins, somewhat hesitantly, to explain her purpose, pleading with Angelo for leniency. When Angelo repeats his firm views, she seems ready to give in – 'O just, but severe law' (line 41), but Lucio urges her to try harder, telling her she is too 'cold' (line 45) in her pleas. She sets to her task of persuasion again with more passion, but Angelo is adamant, arguing that the law 'hath slept' (line 90) but 'now 'tis awake' (line 93) and must therefore be enforced with due severity. As Isabella's oratory becomes more ardent, Lucio and the Provost suggest that her words are having some effect on their hearer, and finally Angelo relents from his absolute position and tells her to return the next day. An **aside** gives an indication of his motives: 'I am that way going to temptation. / Where prayers cross' (lines 158–9). His **soliloquy** expands on this theme, as Angelo muses on his previous immunity to sexual desire and the sudden longings Isabella has provoked in him. For the first time, he understands the vulnerability engendered by desire.

> **CONTEXT**
>
> Shakespeare made use of the soliloquy in a great many of his plays. The best known is the 'To be, or not to be' soliloquy in *Hamlet*.

COMMENTARY

This is an electrifying scene in which two of the play's principals meet and the dynamic between them sets the subsequent action in motion (see **Extended commentaries, Text 2**). It is Angelo's third appearance and, through out the play so far, adjectives such as 'severe' (II.1.269), 'strait in virtue' (II.1.9) and 'precise' (I.3.50) have been attached to him. The Duke's suggestion at the end of I.4 that perhaps this upright, uptight ruler is not all he seems has, however, set up the expectation of Angelo's fall. Here we see it beginning. At the opening of the scene Angelo is all certainty and resolution, signing papers, giving orders, dispensing commands with no thought for the human consequences. At Isabella's entrance, his certainty starts to dissolve. As soon as he sees her he tells the Provost to stay with them – he seems to want more people at the interview. For a while he is able to maintain his own cold equanimity, reiterating arguments about punishment which we have heard in his conversation with Escalus in the previous scene: the answer to the high incidence of crime is not to be lenient but to be more strict, and the fact that the crimes may be those to which figures in authority are themselves susceptible does not mean that they should go unpunished. Isabella's arguments echo those of Escalus but her stress is on mercy as the pre-eminent quality of

authority. Claudio, she says, would be merciful to Angelo were he
guilty of the same crime (see **Themes**, on **Substitution**). (There is
fine **dramatic irony** in the fact that Angelo will commit the same
crime of premarital sex later in the play and that even here in this
scene his thoughts are lustful.) Her language employs the religious
terms 'grace' (lines 62, 78), 'mercy' (lines 50, 63), 'pity' (line 99), and
she talks of the ultimate ruler, God, 'He, which is the top of
judgement' (line 75). She even offers a bribe, using an earthly term
to get Angelo's attention and then promising a spiritual, not
material, bargain from the prayers of 'fasting maids' (line 154) and
the rewards of heaven. Angelo's speeches stress the iniquity of sin
and the punitive side of justice rather than its abstract properties,
using words such as 'condemn' (lines 37–8), 'fault' (lines 39, 40),
'forfeit' (line 71), 'edict' (line 92), 'offence' (line 102), 'foul wrong'
(line 103). For him the law is an absolute; Isabella appeals to a
higher sense of justice.

When Angelo tells her 'your brother is a forfeit of the law' (line 71),
a formulation which implicitly distinguishes himself from the
criminal Claudio, she counters with the Christian idea that 'all the
souls that were were forfeit once' (line 73) before being redeemed
through God's mercy, thus demolishing any moral ground from
which to judge another by asserting that the common inheritance of
humanity is its sinfulness. Having been accused of coldness by
Lucio she has warmed to her persuasive theme, moving from the
specific case of Claudio to a rhetorical disquisition on human
authority and its limitations and dominating the scene through her
eloquence. Angelo is reduced to half-lines or to short, stiffly formal
assertions of his position. Throughout this shift of power, there is
considerable tension and energy between them (see **Extended
commentaries: Text 2**). Angelo's final **soliloquy** is the first time he
is alone on stage and gives us an insight into his character (see
Characterisation). The speech is choppy and full of rhetorical
questions and broken phrases, expressing his attempt to come to
terms with his unfamiliar and powerful response to Isabella. His
lustful feelings run counter to his sense of his own identity, causing
him to question his very self: the question 'What dost thou?' leads
inexorably to 'what art thou?' (line 173) for a man who has built his
whole sense of himself on his chastity and self-restraint. In seeing

CONTEXT

Shakespeare has
deliberately
lessened the
severity of
Claudio's 'crime':
in the sources for
the play, Claudio is
accused of raping
Juliet.

QUESTION

Does the play entirely condemn Angelo's character and behaviour?

Angelo struggle with himself we may feel more sympathy for him as the form of the soliloquy allows us a particular access to his thoughts and emotions. The play rarely affords us such privileged insight into its other characters.

GLOSSARY	
4	**He hath … dream** Claudio has not offended in reality
10	**Under your good correction** correct me if I'm wrong
37	**let it be his fault** eliminate the fault rather than Claudio
59	**longs** belongs
74	**all the souls … once** referring to existence before Christian redemption
79	**man new made** for Christians, God's forgiveness was like a second creation
85	**fowl of season** the bird at the best time for eating
98	**successive degrees** further stages
112	**pelting** insignificant
116	**unwedgeable** so strong it cannot be split by iron wedges
120	**glassy** various glosses have been proposed here, including brittle, transparent, or reflected in a mirror
122	**spleens** this organ was regarded as the seat of laughter
126	**We cannot … ourself** there is no single scale of judgement, as there are different standards for those in authority from those for their inferiors
136	**skins** covers superficially, rather than healing
142	**sense** sensuality
149	**sicles** shekels, coins
150	**stones** jewels
159	**prayers cross** contradict each other, are at cross-purposes
166–8	**That lying … season** under the sun the violet (Isabella) flourishes, while the carrion (Angelo) rots
180	**cunning enemy** the devil

SCENE 3

- The Duke, disguised as a friar, visits Juliet in prison and commends her for her repentance.
- The Duke tells Juliet of Claudio's fate.

The disguised Duke tells the Provost that he is making a charitable visit to the prisoners and gains access to Juliet. The Provost tells him that the father of her unborn baby is to be executed for the deed the next day. Juliet tells the Duke that she loves Claudio and that sex was 'mutually committed' (line 27) (see **Sources**), but she also expresses repentance. Hearing of Claudio's punishment she is horrified.

COMMENTARY

This short scene contrasts with the extended tension of the previous one, and sees the Duke's first entrance in disguise and Juliet's only words (she makes silent appearances in I.2 and V.1). The Duke hears of Angelo's severity in the punishment of Claudio, and he encourages Juliet to repent of her behaviour. His pious observations may suffer from the audience's knowledge that his friar's habit is a disguise rather than a genuine vocation. Juliet is repentant but cuts short the Duke's homily (line 34). In stressing the moral and religious aspect of Juliet's behaviour and her primary allegiance to a religious rather than social law, the Duke may seem to ally himself with Isabella's sense of justice rather than Angelo's.

> **CONTEXT**
>
> The Folio text of the play has 'feard' in line 9 of Angelo's soliloquy. Most editors change it to 'seared' – does this seem a helpful emendation?

GLOSSARY

12	**blistered her report** spoiled her reputation
28	**heavier kind** whether women or men were seen to be most at fault in such matters is unclear; the Duke may be punning on 'heavier' as a description of Juliet's pregnancy
30–4	**lest you … in fear** distinguishing between true repentance arising from love for God, and false repentance prompted by fear of divine punishment
39	***Benedicite*** bless you

**CHECK
THE BOOK**

Harriet Hawkins'
*Measure for
Measure* (1987)
discusses the
conflicting critical
interpretations of
Isabella's character,
including accounts
influenced by
Freudian ideas of
repressed sexuality.

SCENE 4

- Angelo tells Isabella that he will spare Claudio if she agrees to
  have sex with him.

- Isabella threatens to expose Angelo's hypocrisy but he taunts
  that no one will believe her, and she admits the truth of this.

- Isabella reflects that she cannot give up her virtue at any price.

Angelo's **soliloquy** meditates on his struggle between physical
desire and self-restraint, and Isabella's appointed visit is announced.
She is suppliant and it is for him to tell her his decision. He does this
with some circumlocution, quibbling that her brother must die, in
the sense that all people must die, but that his life might be
extended. He comes to the point, offering her a choice between her
brother's execution under 'most just law' (line 52) or her submission
'to such sweet uncleanness / As she that he [Claudio] hath stained'
(lines 54–5). Isabella seems not to understand him, and continues to
beg for Claudio's life. 'I'll speak more gross' (line 82), says Angelo,
and reiterates his terms. Her response is fiery and adamant, and she
asserts that her brother's swift death is preferable to the eternal
damnation of the sin proposed by Angelo. Angelo notes that she
seemed less condemnatory of the fault in Claudio but she argues
that she only excused it for her greater love of her brother. When
he tells her he loves her, Isabella retorts that for the same crime
Claudio is condemned to death (see **Themes**, on **Symmetry and
antithesis**). She tries to regain the upper hand in the scene by
threatening to 'tell the world / What man thou art' (lines 153–4).
Angelo counters that no one will believe such a report because of
his unblotted reputation, and urges her again that her brother's
death will be the result of her refusal to yield to his desires. He tells
her to return the next day with her answer. In Isabella's final speech
after he has left, she recognises that she has no hope of exposing his
hypocrisy. She reflects that Claudio would never want her to agree
to such a bargain for his sake because 'More than our brother is our
chastity' (line 185). She resolves to visit him in prison and 'fit his
mind to death' (line 187).

COMMENTARY

Angelo's last appearance at the end of Scene 2 was in soliloquy; this scene opens with another, giving the impression that he has been struggling with his desires ever since his first interview with Isabella. His speech is oblique and troubled: he states that his words of prayer are empty because 'his invention' (his thoughts) 'Anchors on Isabel' (line 4). Angelo's phrase 'false seeming' (line 15) anticipates Isabella's bitter denunciation 'Seeming, seeming!' (line 150): both echo the Duke's plan in I.3.54, 'what our seemers be', as the truth behind Angelo's seeming propriety has been revealed. Isabella's opening line is problematic. There is a definite, perhaps unwitting, sexual meaning in 'I am come to know your pleasure' (line 31), particularly as it follows Angelo's feverish account of the mounting lust in his blood, and many critics have commented on the imagery of sexual sado-masochism with which she rejects Angelo's proposition: 'Th'impression of keen whips I'd wear as rubies, / And strip myself to death as to a bed / That long I have been sick for' (lines 101–3) (see **Characterisation**). If Isabella's language is subconsciously sexual, however, she is slow to pick up on Angelo's overt approach. The scene is full of tense formulations of equivalence and exchange as both of them explore and assert their individual moral codes, and these can be imagined as oppositions: the soul v. the body, sin v. charity, swift death v. eternal damnation, Isabella's ignorance v. her sexual teasing. All these are versions of and elaborations on the central exchange of sex v. life (see **Themes**, on **Symmetry and antithesis; Substitution**). No compromise or accommodation or negotiation is possible in this clashing of extreme and absolute choices.

Whereas in previous scenes it was Angelo who was always adamant and inflexible, here Isabella assumes that position. At their last interview she made the case for mercy amid the general unworthiness of humanity and here it is Angelo who asserts, as part justification, part recognition, 'We are all frail' (line 121). The scene escalates to a climax in his admission 'now I give my sensual race the rein' (line 160): his time for soul-searching and struggling against temptation is past as he becomes increasingly driven by his desires. Isabella's **soliloquy** – her only one in the play – expresses

CHECK THE BOOK

Actor Juliet Stevenson discusses her interpretation of the character of Isabella in *Clamorous Voices: Shakespeare's Women Today* edited by Carol Rutter (1987).

CHECK THE BOOK

David Crystal's *Shakespeare's Words* (2002) is a great source of information about Shakespeare's language.

her reliance on Claudio's agreeing with her decision. The emotion of the preceding encounter has infused her speech with **hyperbole**: 'had he twenty heads to tender down' (line 180). She resolves on absolutes, delivered in the starkly precise and clipped diction of 'Then, Isabel, live chaste, and, brother, die' (line 185) and her last four lines fall into two **couplets** emphasising the finality of her moral decision.

GLOSSARY	
3	**invention** thought
9	**gravity** propriety, sober living
11	**idle plume** foolish, frivolous feather worn in the hat
12	**place** position of authority
15	**Blood** sexual appetite
16–17	**Let's write … crest** the precise meaning of these lines is unclear, but they elaborate on Angelo's good / evil opposition between 'seeming' and being
19	**Teach** show
45	**coin God's image** produce bastard children (the image is of counterfeit coins)
48	**restrainèd** forbidden
51	**pose** pose a problem
57–8	**Our compelled … accompt** referring to the proverb that 'compelled sins are no sins'
59	**warrant** endorse
73	**nothing of your answer** not something for which you are responsible
79	**black masks** perhaps referring to the black veil worn by the order of St Clare
80	**enshield** defended
90	**in the loss of question** for the sake of argument
97	**supposed** imagined person
111	**Ignomy in ransom** freedom obtained at shameful price
119	**something** somewhat
122	**fedary** confederate
123	**Owe and succeed** own and inherit
127–8	**Men their … by them** men degrade themselves as superior beings when they take advantage of women's frailty

130	**credulous to false prints** another image from counterfeiting, suggesting that women are easily moulded
134	**arrest** take you at
138	**destined livery** the costume of frailty which is the lot of womankind
147	**pluck on others** test others
160	**I give my sensual race the rein** give free rein to my sexual inclinations
162	**nicety** coyness
	prolixious superfluous
163	**banish what they sue for** are so alluring they heighten rather than appease the lover's desires
174	**approof** approval
178	**prompture** prompting
180	**tender down** lay down in payment

 CHECK THE NET

Have a look at William Holman Hunt's Pre-Raphaelite painting 'Claudio and Isabella' at **www.tate.org.uk.** Which lines in the scene do you think it represents?

ACT III

SCENE 1

- The 'friar'/Duke urges Claudio to prepare himself for death.
- Isabella tells Claudio about Angelo's proposition, and while he is initially horrified, he tries to persuade her to do it to save his life.
- Isabella leaves angrily.
- The Duke tells Claudio that Angelo is only testing Isabella and there is no hope of a pardon.
- Claudio repents his treatment of his sister.
- The Duke unfolds to Isabella a plan to resolve the situation: Angelo's jilted sweetheart Mariana will take Isabella's place.

At the beginning of the scene, Claudio professes himself 'prepared to die' (line 4), and the Duke, in his role as friar, delivers a long speech on the worthlessness of life and the folly of holding it so dear. All life is fear of death, he preaches, and therefore death should be sought as an early release from this servitude. Claudio repeats his sentiments of resignation to his fate. This is an important prelude to the encounter with Isabella, in which Claudio's stoicism is rapidly contradicted by his attempts to save his own life through his sister. Isabella enters and offers her brother the comfort of his imminent trip to heaven. In response to his asking whether there is any alternative, she admits that there is but that it is at a price too high. She explains Angelo's proposition, beginning to doubt her brother's response as she does so. He agrees that she should not sacrifice herself in this way. Gradually, however, the possibility of his escape dawns on him, and he begins to suggest that it would not be a sin to save his life. He speaks eloquently of the terrors of death, 'to die, and go we know not where, / To lie in cold obstruction and to rot' (lines 121–2) in contrast to his earlier resignation. Isabella is angry at his suggestion and leaves. The Duke intervenes to have some private conversation with her, first telling Claudio that he has heard Angelo's confession and knows that his proposal to Isabella is only a trick and that there is no hope of his sentence being lifted. He must prepare himself for death. Claudio wishes pardon from his sister for his behaviour. Then the Duke tells Isabella of his plan. Angelo had been engaged to marry a woman named Mariana, whose brother was drowned along with her dowry, before the wedding. Hearing that she had no riches to bring him, Angelo broke off the engagement under the guise of having heard some rumours about his fiancée's morality and character. Despite this cruelty, however, Mariana maintains her love for her erstwhile sweetheart. The Duke proposes that Isabella go along with Angelo's scheme and set a place for them to meet. There they will interpose Mariana in her place, and then put pressure on Angelo to marry her with the revelation that he has already slept with her. Isabella agrees with this plan.

> **CONTEXT**
>
> Many critics have compared Claudio's speeches on death to those of Hamlet, especially the famous 'To be, or not to be' soliloquy.

COMMENTARY

This long scene is packed with incident, revelation and emotion, all pivoting on the activities of the disguised Duke. In his sermon about the meaning of life delivered to Claudio, he urges him to 'Be absolute for death' (line 5), encouraging the hapless prisoner in the kind of absolute certainty and single-mindedness which has already been seen to motivate both Angelo and Isabella. The Duke's discourse uses many examples and images to persuade his listener of the futility of a life spent in the shadow of death. The language is reductive, humans are merely 'death's fool' (line 11), consisting of 'many a thousand grains / That issue out of dust' (lines 20–1). The speech is crammed with negatives, with the repeated phrase 'thou art not' (lines 13, 19 and 23) echoed in 'Thou'rt by no means' (line 15), 'Thou hast not' (line 36), and 'Thou hast neither' (line 37). This catalogue of reasons why death is actually to be preferred over life stresses the burden of existence, in contrast to Claudio's subsequent speech in lines 121–35 which focuses, in panic and despair, on the fearful and unknown passage of death itself. The Duke's philosophy of stoicism is markedly unsuited to his friar's costume: where Christian religion might well preach the futility of life on earth, it does so with reference to the greater glories of the afterlife. There is no mention of judgement or life after death in the Duke's long speech, and because he delivers it from his disguised position, it is hard to know quite how to read it. For Roger Allam, who played the Duke in the 1987 production of the play by the Royal Shakespeare Company, this passage was crucial to his whole idea of his character: 'I found that if I related the lines to myself as much as to Claudio the speech was unlocked for me, and a central part of the Duke's character fell into place. His sense of self has fragmented into "many a thousand grains" of dust …. In a sense the purpose of the Duke's journey through the play so far is to realise completely his own sceptical fatalism. But somehow this can only be expressed through someone else's situation' (see **Critical history**; **Characterisation**). This argues that the Duke's words, so cheerless to the man who is staring death in the face, are revelatory about his own personality at this point in the play. The truth of the speech is, however, subtly distorted by the fact of the Duke's disguise and his wider, but as yet undelivered, plans that Claudio shall not in fact die and that therefore the question of his preparedness for death is irrelevant.

It is important that the Duke overhears Isabella's conversation with her brother, for it is here that news of Angelo's hypocrisy reaches him. Isabella and Claudio's speeches make an interesting pattern. Her speeches end on half-lines, as at lines 63, 65, 70, 73, 76, 84 and

CHECK THE BOOK

Robert Watson's essay on the play, reprinted in Smith (ed.) *Blackwell Guides to Criticism: Shakespeare's Comedies* (2003), discusses the implications of its closeness to death, the subject matter associated with tragedy.

97, and their metrical incompleteness registers both what is left
unsaid in her account and a space for him to speak, almost as if she
is leaving him a metrical gap in which to reassure her. Instead his
responses are increasingly panicky questions, hurrying the story
along and clutching at straws (see **Extended commentaries, Text 3**).
She discloses the situation in incremental pieces, and her speech
seesaws, like much of the scene, on the words 'life' and 'death'. 'Yes,
brother,' she announces, 'you may live' (line 67) and again the
cropped line leaves a gap for Claudio's reaction, before she resumes
her analysis that such a life would 'fetter you till death' (line 70). As
in her discussion with Angelo in II.4, Isabella's perspective on
justice is a religious one, and here again her interlocutor has more
earthly preoccupations. The comfort she brings is not mortal but
heavenly. Claudio interprets her imagery of 'fetters', by which she
suggests the fettering of the immortal soul in sin, literally, as
'Perpetual durance' – life imprisonment – and in response Isabella
takes back this literal interpretation as a religious **metaphor**. She
seems, as he observes fretfully, unable to come to the point plainly,
and she admits that she fears to do so. When she does tell him, she is
encouraged by his vehemence, but having been given an option of
freedom at whatever price he begins to haver. Like Angelo at
II.4.63–4, Claudio attempts to realign moral edicts, arguing for a
relative rather than an absolute concept of sin: 'Sure it is no sin, /
Or of the deadly seven it is the least' (lines 113–14). In his speech on
death as 'too horrible' (line 131), Claudio's imagery is all of matter
and the elements, of the 'warm motion' (line 124) turned to 'cold
obstruction' (line 123), of the body imprisoned in fire or ice or
winds: like the Duke he has no confidence in an afterlife, still less in
a heaven or in God's mercy, but his response is to find 'most loathèd
worldly life' (line 132) 'a paradise' (line 134) by comparison. It is a
powerful speech with echoes of Hamlet's attempts to make a
meaning of his life, and establishes Claudio as a character of real
depth and interest (see **Characterisation**).

Isabella shows no compassion for his fears when set against the
price which is demanded for his life, nor does she revert to the
Christian concept of comfort with which she began the interview.
Her exclamatory denunciations mark her fury and her brother's
attempts to continue the conversation are disregarded. Isabella's

**CHECK
THE FILM**

The BBC 1978 film
uses a close-up of
Isabella and Claudio
embracing while he
initially supports her
response to
Angelo's
proposition. It
symbolises the
increasing distance
between them by
showing them
separate and facing
away from each
other in Claudio's
cell.

discomfiture at her brother's response carries into her initial words
with the Duke, where she snappishly tells him she has 'no
superfluous leisure' (line 160). Both speak in prose, perhaps to
register a relaxation of the tension notched up by the tautly
interlaced pentameters of the preceding encounter. The Duke's
remarks to Claudio are terse and to the point, and, as an audience,
we may wonder momentarily whether we ought to believe him.
This confusion emphasises the ambiguity of the Duke's character
(see **Characterisation**). His intervention to confirm to Isabella that
Claudio's death is imminent seems an unnecessary cruelty at a point
when we do not know his overall strategy.

The conversation between the Duke and Isabella conveys a good
deal of important plot information, including the introduction of
Mariana as a device to solve the tangled situation. The Duke speaks
the most, moving matters quickly along, hardly allowing any space
for Isabella to question this dubious plan. His orders are clear and
detailed, full of imperative verbs of command, almost breathless in
their speed and length. The plan demonstrates a level of physical
and mental energy that the Duke has not hitherto revealed. At this
point he turns from a man who has been characterised by impotence
and inactivity, who has let things slip, abdicated his position and
taken up the passive role of observer in his own state, into an
authoritative figure in active control of an audacious and exciting plot
(see **Characterisation**). He takes Isabella, who seems dazed by her
encounter with Claudio and who speaks only a few lines, all
characterised by indignant and exclamatory rhetoric, along with him.
The scene plays daringly with improbability – why would Isabella
agree to place Mariana in a position she so vehemently rejects for
herself? Paola Dionisotti, who played Isabella in a production in
1978, argues that the scene works because 'she is so devastated by
what has just happened – that horrendous scene with her brother in
which everything is severed and smashed – that she is like putty in the
Duke's hands. He is madly constructing some framework, throwing
some desperate lifeline which, *because* of her desperation, she grabs'
(see **Critical history; Characterisation**). There is some **dramatic
irony** in her vow to tell the Duke, when he returns, how mistaken he
has been about Angelo's character. **Peripeteia**, the turn of the plot for
the good, is in sight.

CONTEXT

As in the case of
the magician
Prospero in *The
Tempest,* the
Duke's power to
arrange events
and script a drama
has often been
associated with
the art of the
playwright.

www. CHECK THE NET

An online version of the First Folio text, good for searching, is available at **www.etext. virginia.edu/ shakespeare/folio/**

In the Folio text there is no scene break at this point, leaving the whole of Act III without a scene change. Scene changes in the Renaissance theatre were prompted by a momentarily empty stage when all the actors from one episode leave to be replaced by a different set of characters. As the Duke remains on stage between Isabella's exit at line 269 and the entrance of Elbow, Pompey and Officers in the next line, there is a clear logic to the Folio arrangement. Played or read without a scene break the sense of the action speeding up would be enhanced.

GLOSSARY	
10	keep'st dwell
12–13	For him … him still you try to run away from death but you are always running towards it
14	accommodations conveniences
16	fork forked tongue
17	worm snake
18	provok'st invites
23	certain constant
29	bowels offspring, children
	do call thee sire acknowledge you as father
31	rheum catarrh, discharge
36	palsied eld old people afflicted by palsy
37	heat energy
	limb strength
62	lieger resident ambassador
63	appointment preparations
64	set on begin a journey
70	Perpetual durance life imprisonment
73	determined scope defined limit
75	bark strip bark from
92	appliances remedies
94	enew drive into the water (the image is from falconry)
96	cast scoured, purged
99	invest clothe
100	guards decorative facings or trimmings on the front of a garment

118	**perdurably fined** eternally punished
124	**delighted** capable of feeling delight
126	**thrilling** piercing
129	**pendent** hanging, floating
140	**dishonest** lewd, dishonourable
144	**shield** forbid
145	**warpèd slip** contorted shoot, immoral son
	wilderness wildness
146	**defiance** contempt, enmity
157	**dispense** give up
165–6	**practise … natures** test his ability as a judge of character
185	**complexion** nature
191	**resolve** answer
195	**government** moral conduct and political rule
198	**avoid** refute
212	**miscarried** died through an accident
224	**combinate** betrothed
235	**avail** benefit
246	**refer yourself to this advantage** place this condition
251	**stead up** fulfil
256	**frame** direct, prepare

 QUESTION

Is it reasonable that both Isabella and Mariana both accept the Duke's plan?

Scene 2

- The disguised Duke denounces Pompey who has been rearrested.
- Lucio refuses to stand bail for Pompey, and then, in conversation with the 'friar', he slanders the absent Duke as a drunken libertine.
- Mistress Overdone, also in custody, accuses Lucio of having a child with a woman outside marriage.
- Escalus praises the Duke to the 'friar', and expresses concern for Claudio.

Elbow's reappearance with the still unrepentant and jesting Pompey gives the Duke the chance to address one of his reprobate subjects from the position of his disguise. His denunciation is fierce, and he seems almost to forget himself as friar in the ducal order 'Take him to prison, officer' (line 29). Lucio banters with Pompey, using his name repeatedly in ironic mockery of its noble associations, and bids him off to prison as a bawd. He refuses to be Pompey's bail. When the prison party has exited, Lucio engages the 'friar' in conversation about the absent Duke and about Angelo's behaviour as his deputy. They both agree that Angelo is too severe, and Lucio jokes that he is not even human, so cold is he to physical pleasures. Lucio criticises Angelo's harsh punishment of Claudio, and asserts that the Duke would not have been so sharp, for 'He had some feeling for the sport' (line 113). The Duke tries to defend himself but Lucio claims an intimacy with the Duke which gives him insight into his foibles, adding 'He would be drunk too' (line 121) and that he was not in fact wise as he was held to be, but rather 'very superficial, ignorant, unweighing' (line 132). The Duke finds out Lucio's name. The conversation then turns to Claudio's fate, but this Lucio also brings round to the supposed cupidity of the Duke. When he has left, the Duke speaks angrily of 'back-wounding calumny' (line 176). Mistress Overdone enters in the guard of the officers and Escalus. She begs Escalus for mercy but he is adamant in his sentencing. She says that it is Lucio who has informed on her, and makes a counter-accusation that he has fathered a child with Kate Keepdown. Escalus calls for Lucio to be summoned and despatches her to prison. Escalus exchanges some words with the disguised Duke, who states that the world is in a critical condition because goodness is in such short supply. The Duke asks Escalus 'of what disposition was the Duke?' (lines 220–1), and receives a more comfortable answer about the Duke's temperance and sobriety. They discuss Claudio's demeanour in the face of death. The Duke's final **soliloquy** reflects on Angelo's hypocritical behaviour and on the need to employ 'Craft against vice' (line 265) to bring about a just conclusion.

CHECK THE BOOK

In his *The Empty Space*, first published in 1977, radical theatre director Peter Brook discusses his production: 'When this play is prettily staged, it is meaningless – it demands an absolutely convincing roughness and dirt.'

COMMENTARY

This scene seems designed to amplify and corroborate for the Duke the news of Angelo's corruption, and to demonstrate the general failings of humanity. In parading the reprobate citizens Pompey and Mistress Overdone and giving voice to Lucio's defamatory opinions of the Duke, this episode prompts the disguised ruler to reflect on the sinful state of humanity. The scene is punctuated with his remarks on the prevailing moral climate, from his injunction to Pompey 'Go mend, go mend' (line 25), to his inclusive **couplet** on the gap between seeming and genuine virtue: 'That we were all, as some would seem to be, / Free from our faults, as faults from seeming free' (lines 36–7). In his guise as the friar he tells Escalus that 'there is so great a fever on goodness' (line 212) everywhere, and his response to Lucio's cheery descriptions of a rakish Duke is the bitter recognition that 'calumny / The whitest virtue strikes' (lines 176–7). Everywhere he looks, he seems to see sinfulness and moral depravity and a profound lack of respect for authority. Even the prose in which the scene is largely written, apart from a few lines of the Duke's, seems to signal a decline in standards and a relaxation of formal rules paralleling the moral degeneracy of the characters. The Duke's final speech is written in short-lined rhyming couplets which stand out from the rest of the play – such that many earlier critics considered them, without any external justification, to be a non-Shakespearean interpolation. In their **gnomic**, sometimes obscure pronouncements, they develop the Duke's character (see **Characterisation**) and present him as a **choric** observer of past events and their ethical charge as well as an active shaper of the future. They move from supplying general maxims about good government to reflections on Angelo's degraded character and an unusually explicit declaration in the final four lines about what the rest of the play will enact.

Much of the scene's tension and humour derives from the **dramatic irony** of the other characters' ignorance that this 'friar' is in fact the absented Duke. Lucio unknowingly digs himself deeper and deeper into a hole as he lists the Duke's flaws. How to assess this new perspective on the Duke is difficult. It does not coincide with anything previously stated about his character, although it does provide an explanation – and no alternative explanation is offered – for why the Duke was able to preside over such a protracted descent into vice and lawlessness. Even Escalus's counterview does not quite erase the strength of Lucio's confident slanders, although his

> **CONTEXT**
>
> In Shakespearean plays, prose is often used to show that the speaker is morally or socially inferior.

considered view that the Duke's prime concern was 'to know himself' offers another insight into his character (see **Characterisation**). The Duke's incognito encounter with his people does not reflect the image of himself which he desires. Spurred on by what he has learnt through his disguise, he ends the third act of the play with a definite plan of action: the relatively passive, distracted man of the first two acts has taken surreptitious control of the play.

QUESTION

Where would you put the interval in a performance of *Measure for Measure*? Why?

GLOSSARY	
3	bastard sweet Spanish wine
5	two usuries moneylending and prostitution
8	fox fox fur was associated with moneylenders
38	cord hangman's rope and the girdle which is part of the friar's habit
43	Pygmalion's images in classical mythology, Pygmalion brought his statues to life by falling in love with them. The image suggests fresh young women whose looks are unspoiled
44–5	extracting it clutched stealing a purse, or perhaps suggesting masturbation
46	tune fashion
54	tub (pun) barrel in which beef is salted; the sweating tub used for the treatment of venereal disease
67	husband housekeeper
75	paint use cosmetics
88	fantastical irrational
97	extirp root out, extinguish
103	stockfishes dried cod
105	motion generative sexless puppet
109	codpiece baggy flap worn over hose or breeches at the groin, hence the male genitals
120	clack-dish begging bowl, perhaps with a sexual innuendo
124	inward intimate friend
130	greater file of the subject majority of the populace
132	unweighing unthinking, lacking in judgement
134	helmed directed
162	tun-dish funnel, with a sexual pun

163	**ungenitured** without genitals
169	**untrussing** untying the lower garments, or urinating
171	**eat mutton on Fridays** religious laws forbade the eating of meat on Friday
	mutton prostitute
172	**mouth** kiss
173	**brown bread** coarse bread
190	**information** legal complaint or charge
193	**Philip and Jacob** the saints' day falls on 1 May
200	**brother** fellow, colleague
214–16	**it is as … any undertaking** the meaning seems to be that inconstancy is now a virtue
222	**strifes** objectives
232	**sinister** unjust
240	**shore** limit
258	**my vice** the vice I have allowed to flourish
261–4	**How may … things** cryptic, possibly corrupt lines from which only the most general sense of the Duke's fulmination against hypocrisy can be deduced
270	**perform** bring to fruition
	contracting betrothal

ACT IV

SCENE 1

- The Duke introduces Isabella to Mariana.
- The details of how Isabella has arranged to meet Angelo are revealed.
- Assured by the 'friar' that her compliance is no sin, Mariana agrees to the plan.

The scene begins with music and lyrics which seem to emphasise unrequited love. The Duke arrives in his friar's disguise, in which he

www. CHECK THE NET

Mariana captivated nineteenth century artists including Tennyson, whose poem 'Mariana' can be found at **www. library.utoronto. ca/utel/rp/poems/ tennyson1.html** and Dante Gabriel Rossetti whose painting can be see at **www. abcgallery.com/ R/rossetti/rossetti 36/html**.

has clearly often visited Mariana to act as her comforter (see **Treatment of time**), and they exchange some words. The Duke indicates he may need to speak further with Mariana. Isabella comes with news of her planned rendezvous with the lustful Angelo that night at the gate of his walled garden. The plan is moving ahead, but Mariana still knows nothing of it. The Duke indicates that Isabella will tell her, and the two women withdraw for the discussion. The Duke briefly reflects again on rank and worth. Isabella and Mariana return, having agreed the plan. Isabella reminds her to mention Claudio as she leaves Angelo, and the Duke reassures her that as 'He is your husband on a pre-contract' (line 71) there is no sin involved in the deed.

COMMENTARY

Mariana's agreement to the plan is crucial to the success of the Duke's machinations, and here she gives no demur. Nor does Isabella, to whom the job of presenting the proposal is delegated by the Duke. Both these acceptances are strange, and draw attention to the play's governing symmetry (see **Themes**, on **Symmetry and antithesis**). For Mariana is being asked to behave as Juliet has and for which Juliet is being punished. The premarital betrothal which Claudio claimed for himself and Juliet in I.2.144–8 has provided no mitigation for his offence, but here the existence of the same kind of contract between Mariana and Angelo is held to justify their sexual liaison. What was a capital sin in Claudio is 'no sin' (line 72) for Mariana. Isabella's willingness to connive with this plan adds to the complexity of her moral character (see **Characterisation**), and she expresses no squeamishness at all about retaining her own chastity at the expense of another woman's. She even reminds Mariana to mention 'her brother' (line 69) when she leaves Angelo's bed. Mariana's own characterisation in the scene is sketchy. She speaks only a few lines, and those which have the potential to be the most interesting, her response to the plan, are not heard. It seems a deliberate marginalisation of her as a human being: she is just a function, another body (see **Themes**, on **Substitution**), in whom we cannot afford to become too interested or her role will become too difficult to sustain. The Duke ends the scene, as he did Act III, with another promise of active resolution, using the natural imagery of fruition and harvest previously used by Lucio to describe Claudio

CONTEXT

Shakespeare uses a similar 'bed-trick' plot in *All's Well that Ends Well*, a play often compared with *Measure for Measure* as a problem play.

and Juliet's affair (I.4.40–4), serving again to emphasise the parallels between Angelo and Mariana and Claudio and Juliet.

GLOSSARY	
27	circummured walled around
29	planchèd planked
30	his its
39	all of precept by verbal instruction (i.e. not by taking her there)
41	observance compliance
42	repair visit
43	possessed told
	most utmost, longest
46	stays waits
61	contrarious quests conflicting enquiries
62	escapes outbursts
64	rack distort, misinterpret
71	pre-contract a contract of marriage
74	flourish decorate

SCENE 2

- In the prison, Pompey is appointed to assist the executioner Abhorson.
- Angelo's order to execute Claudio is reiterated: his head is to be sent to Angelo in the morning.
- The disguised Duke persuades the Provost to spare Claudio and instead send the head of Barnadine, a convicted murderer.

CONTEXT

Abhorson's name is a bawdy pun combining 'abhor', 'whore's son', and, it has been suggested, 'abortion'.

The Provost arranges for Pompey to assist the executioner Abhorson at the executions of Claudio and Barnadine in return for a reduction of his sentence. Abhorson exchanges a few laconic words with his new assistant who is still full of puns and bawdy jokes. The Provost expresses his pity for Claudio, but not for Barnadine as a murderer. Claudio tells him that Barnadine is sleeping, and the Provost wishes Claudio comfort as he prepares for his death. The Duke in his friar's disguise comes to visit the Provost, and defends Angelo's actions as the 'great justice' of one who is innocent of the crimes he punishes in others, allowing that 'Were he mealed with that / Which he corrects, then were he tyrannous' (lines 81–2). The Duke tells the Provost that a pardon for Claudio is likely to arrive, and, on cue, a messenger appears. The Duke appears to anticipate that Angelo will keep his side of the bargain, having slept, as he believes, with Isabella. The message, however, is that Claudio is to be executed by four o'clock and that his head is to be sent to Angelo within an hour. The Duke asks the Provost about Barnadine's situation and character, and hears that this prisoner is impenitent of his crime and has no fear of death. The Duke tells the Provost to spare Claudio's life and execute Barnadine, and to send his head, shaved to look more like that of Claudio, to Angelo. The Provost demurs at this action which 'is against my oath' (line 176), but the Duke persuades him that the Duke, to whom the Provost swore his oath, would approve his actions and shows him a letter with the ducal seal and signature to add weight to this promise. He continues to persuade and reassure him.

 QUESTION

The Duke is not a godlike figure, or a benign presence, but an unsympathetic and deceiving bungler. Do you agree?

COMMENTARY

In this prison scene we see the Duke's plans coming closer to fruition, as he introduces the expedient device of sending another man's head in place of Claudio's (see **Themes**, on **Substitution**). The first half of the scene is concerned with the dark humour of the interchange between the pointedly named Abhorson (his name puns on 'abhor' as well as on 'whore's son') and the irrepressible Pompey. Pompey makes much merriment on a joke linking beheading with the taking of women's maidenheads, or virginity, thereby allying his current and former occupations. The true cost of this 'mystery' or executioner's craft is demonstrated with Claudio's short appearance. He says nothing about himself or his own feelings as he waits for morning and death: after his anguished eloquence in III.1 he seems spent, and he does not speak again in the play after this short interchange with the Provost. The Duke's entrance is cheery – inappropriately so – and he seems to be enjoying his new active role in setting the tangled situation to rights. His speech about Angelo's justness as a man who punishes crimes and appetites which he himself restrains is heavily ironic: the Duke and the audience know that this is far from the truth. His apparent defence of the deputy, therefore, is an implicit accusation. His response to Angelo's message about Claudio's execution shows him thinking quickly and creatively. Having expected a pardon, he quickly regains control of events as he establishes the suitability of Barnadine as a substitute for Claudio. His long prose speeches show him talking over any opposition to his plans, as he did when proposing the bed-trick plan to Isabella in III.1. The Duke overrides the Provost's misgivings with the authority of the (supposedly absent) Duke. For the first time in the play, therefore, we see the Duke use his authority, albeit by a kind of proxy, and this may mark a promise of more active and just government in the future. References to the dawn at the end of the scene draw attention to the quickening time-scale of events (see **Treatment of time**).

GLOSSARY	
4	wife's head (pun) the man as head of the household, and 'maidenhead' = 'virginity'
6	snatches jokes
11	gyves shackles, fetters
21	compound make terms
26	mystery profession
40–4	Every true … your thief a garbled exposition based on the hangman's traditional right to the clothes of his victims, and punning on 'fits' = 'is the right size for' and 'is appropriate to'
	good turn 'turning off' was the act of execution
64	starkly stiffly
77	Even with in conformity with
80	mealed stained
86	unsisting unassisting
	postern back gate or door
95	siege seat
114	putting on urging, incitement
128	nine years old for nine years continued

CONTEXT

Hanging was not abolished in Britain till 1965.

133	**fact** crime
142	**desperately mortal** in a desperate state of mortal sin
168	**discover the favour** recognise the face
184	**attempt** persuade
187	**character** handwriting
196	**unfolding star** morning star
202	**resolve** reassure

SCENE 3

- Barnadine, drunk and unrepentant, refuses to attend his execution.
- The head of Ragozine who has died of fever is to be sent to Angelo in place of that of Claudio.
- The Duke plans to summon Angelo to meet him on his 'return' the next day.
- The Duke tells Isabella that Claudio has been executed, and arranges for her to meet the Duke next day to denounce Angelo publicly.

 CHECK THE NET

The Clink prison, near to Shakespeare's theatre and the origin of the expression 'in the clink' has a website which gives some sense of conditions in early modern prisons: **www.clink.co.uk**.

Pompey gives a disreputable commentary on the prison inmates and he and Abhorson call Barnadine for his execution. With much cursing Barnadine indicates his unpreparedness: 'I have been drinking all night. I am not fitted for't' (lines 41–2). The Duke attempts to persuade him but Barnadine is adamant, and it is decided that it would be 'damnable' – both for Barnadine and for his captors – to execute him while he is in this unrepentant mood. Fortunately, the Provost can reveal that there has been a death from illness in the prison, that of Ragozine, 'a most notorious pirate' (line 69) and a man who even resembles Claudio in colouring. He suggests that Ragozine's head should be sent as Claudio's, and the Duke agrees that this opportunity is heaven-sent. He persuades the Provost to keep both Barnadine and Claudio from execution, promising that within two days the rightness of the course of action will be proved. The Duke plans to send letters announcing his return and bidding one Varrius to meet him to arrange his return. The Provost is despatched to Angelo with the head.

Isabella arrives at the prison to ask for her brother. In a brief **soliloquy** prompted by her approach, the Duke reveals that he 'will keep her ignorant of her good' (line 108). Instead he tells Isabella that Claudio has been executed and his head sent to Angelo. She cannot believe this at first, but the Duke proposes a focus for her anger – the return of the Duke the next day. He bids her go and meet him at the city gate and she will gain 'revenges' (line 134). He also sends her with a letter to Friar Peter bidding him come to Mariana's house. He leaves Isabella in the care of Friar Peter, telling her that he himself will not be present at the Duke's return as he is 'combinèd by a sacred vow' (line 142). Lucio enters, and commiserates with Isabella, stating that if the 'old fantastical Duke of dark corners had been at home' (lines 155–6), Claudio would not have been executed. Lucio tells the disguised Duke more about the character of the Duke, and admits that, being brought before him on a charge of getting a woman pregnant, he denied it.

COMMENTARY

The Duke's plans continue apace. When Isabella complies 'I am directed by you' (line 135), her statement has a more extensive reference than her immediate orders from the friar. The Duke's active control of the plot has subsumed all action by other characters, who seem reduced to trusting to this mysterious 'friar' and carrying out his commands. Isabella, in particular, is a shadow of her former vociferous and assertive self (see **Characterisation**). One character, however, bucks this submissive trend. Barnadine's uncompromising refusal to be executed blocks the Duke's plans and poses a challenge to his plotting. Barnadine declines to be a piece in the Duke's jigsaw, and his unrepentant and unbowed presence in the scene offers a radical alternative to the pious observations of the Duke and Provost. He gains a stay of execution through this determination, but the Duke's plans are hardly interrupted because of the happy coincidence of Ragozine's death. Ragozine enters the play as the substitute for a substitute (see **Themes**, on **Substitution**),

> **CONTEXT**
>
> Pirates seem to have been a handy, if unlikely, plot device for Shakespeare: he uses them in *Hamlet* and in *Pericles* for similarly fortuitous purposes as here.

CHECK THE BOOK

Kate Chedgzoy's account of the play in the 'Writers and their Work' series (2000) is an accessible and sophisticated introduction to its themes.

but the ease of this second replacement casts Barnadine's role into interesting relief. A more streamlined plot would have excised Barnadine's part altogether: if all that is needed is a dead head to stand in for that of Claudio's, the final solution, that of Ragozine's death from fever, would be ideal, without any need for the added complication of Barnadine. That this simpler course was not chosen by Shakespeare means that Barnadine's role is important not primarily as a plot device but as a challenge to the play's prevailing codes of repentance of crime and submission to authority. His behaviour amplifies Pompey's jaunty volubility earlier in the scene and makes his ultimate fate in Act V all the more significant. There are some characters who, it seems, will never submit to the moral or social authority of those in power (see **Themes**, on **Crime, punishment and justice**).

GLOSSARY	
2	house of profession brothel
4	commodity usurers, whose profits were limited by law, increased them by paying some of the loan as commodities which the borrower was supposed to sell to realise the cash. Frequently, as in Master Rash's case, the commodities were of low value and difficult to sell
4	brown paper coarse paper
5	marks a mark was worth 13s. 4d.
11	peaches impeaches
15	tilter jouster
17	doers in our trade clients of the brothel
39	clap into hurry with
46	ghostly father confessor
53	billets sticks
61	ward cell
71	omit leave aside
77	prefixed stipulated
82	continue preserve
87	journal daily
	yond generation perhaps referring to those beyond the dark prison
98	cold gradation gradually and deliberately

117	**close** silent
128	**instance** indication
133	**your bosom** your wishes
140	**perfect** tell the full story
141	**to the head** in front
143	**combinèd** bound
151	**fain** forced
152	**for my head** for fear of being beheaded
155	**fantastical** eccentric, whimsical
160	**woodman** hunter, chaser after women
170	**medlar** prostitute

QUESTION

Measure for Measure was listed under 'comedies' on the contents page when it was first published. Do you agree that it belongs to this category?

SCENE 4

- Angelo and Escalus discuss the Duke's letters, which instruct them to meet him at the city gates.

- Angelo soliloquises on actions he believes he has committed in having sex with Isabella and having Claudio executed.

Angelo and Escalus discuss the Duke's 'uneven and distracted' (line 2) letters and Angelo expresses the hope that 'his wisdom be not tainted' (lines 3–4). They are commanded to proclaim the Duke's return and that if 'any crave redress of injustice' (line 8) they are to do so publicly at that time. Escalus observes that this is to protect his deputies against complaints later. Alone, Angelo fears that the 'deflowered maid' (line 19) may use this opportunity to denounce him, but comforts himself with the thought of his own authority which is immune to scandal. Angelo goes on to express regret at Claudio's death: 'Would yet he had lived' (line 30).

COMMENTARY

Angelo has not been on stage since the end of Act II: this scene shows something of his response to his subsequent actions. The news of the Duke's arrangements for his return throws Angelo into guilty anxiety. Will Isabella take advantage of the Duke's proclamation to condemn him? But while Angelo's primary concern is for his own escape from censure, this **soliloquy** is revelatory of his divided feelings. He cannot quite bring himself to admit to what he believes he has done, preferring the third-person circumlocution of 'by an eminent body that enforced / The law against it' (lines 20–1), but this evasive formulation does recognise the hypocrisy of his behaviour. Again, it seems that Angelo cannot bring himself to speak the name of Claudio, or perhaps his thoughts do not need such labels, but he does seem to admit that his death was wrong. The final **couplet** sums up Angelo's disjointed response: 'we would, and we would not' (line 32) (see **Characterisation**).

GLOSSARY

1	**disvouched** contradicted	
5	**reliver** hand over	
10	**dispatch** prompt settlement	
15	**of sort and suit** those of rank and in attendance	
18	**unshapes me** destroys my self-possession	
	unpregnant unready	
20	**eminent body** public figure	
23	**dares her no** she would not dare	
24	**credent bulk** weighty and respectable	
25	**particular** personal	
27	**sense** sensuality	

SCENE 5

- The Duke instructs Friar Peter who is helping arrange the public denunciation.

The Duke appears in his own clothing and makes plans for his return. He sends Friar Peter to gather together various individuals for this grand repossession of his ducal authority.

CONTEXT

This structural device of a series of short scenes works to speed up the pace of the action. The Jacobean theatre had almost no scenery and few props so such rapid changes of location could be easily managed.

COMMENTARY

The Duke continues to give orders as the sequence of short scenes speeds up the pace of the play towards its **dénouement**. He stresses to Friar Peter that he must keep faith with his plan, although we are not given any details of how the Duke intends to conduct his public interview with Angelo or how matters will be resolved.

GLOSSARY	
1	**deliver me** deliver for me
3	**keep** follow
5	**blench** deviate
6	**minister** suggest

SCENE 6

- Isabella discusses the 'friar's' plan with Mariana.
- Isabella has misgivings about accusing Angelo of having had sex with her.

QUESTION

What is the significance of the play's title to its plot and themes?

Isabella wants Mariana to accuse Angelo, but has been instructed by the disguised Duke to do it herself. She has been reassured that all will come right, even if the 'friar' seems to oppose her. Friar Peter arrives with news that they have an excellent position in the crowd from which to address the Duke. The trumpets have announced that he will very soon enter the gates of the city.

COMMENTARY

In the previous scene the Duke urged Friar Peter to stick to the plan even if events seem to be going against them. Here Isabella indicates that she has been given similar advice by the 'friar'. Both scenes serve to raise the tension about how the play will be resolved, and with these hints about how the final showdown will be managed, the stage is set for the culmination of the Duke's plotting. Mariana's advice 'Be ruled by him' (line 4) emphasises the Duke's control of events: whereas earlier Isabella had been his accomplice in persuading Mariana to his plan now she is ignorant – reduced to one of the pawns the Duke is moving on the great chessboard of his strategy.

GLOSSARY

4	**to veil full purpose** to conceal the plan
10	**stand** position
13	**generous** highest ranking
14	**hent** reached
	near upon shortly

ACT V

SCENE 1

- Back in his rightful clothes, and before a crowd of people, the Duke meets Angelo and Escalus at the city gate, and the truth about Angelo is revealed.
- Angelo is commanded to marry Mariana, and the Duke agrees to spare his life when Isabella and Mariana plead for mercy.
- Claudio is brought in and reminded to marry Juliet.
- Lucio is sentenced to death but this is commuted to marrying Kate Keepdown.
- The Duke proposes marriage to Isabella.

CHECK THE FILM

In the BBC film of 1978, Claudio is brought in wearing the black hood of execution. When it is removed, he embraces Isabella. Juliet enters carrying their baby – and all are happily reunited. Is this how you see it?

The Duke returns and is greeted by Angelo and Escalus and a crowd of other citizens. He congratulates them on their conduct of government during his absence, and announces that he has heard much good of their 'justice'. He makes a speech of public thanks to Angelo. Isabella, prompted by Friar Peter, addresses the Duke and begs him to hear her story and give her justice. The Duke replies that she should seek this from Angelo, but she begs him. Angelo tries to pre-empt her by indicating to the Duke that she may be mad. Isabella denounces Angelo as 'An hypocrite, a virgin-violator' (line 41). The Duke seems to dismiss her, but her story gains his interest and she gives the details of Claudio's fate. Lucio attempts to intervene but is repeatedly silenced by the Duke. The Duke makes to send Isabella to prison, and calls for the 'meddling friar' who has prompted her to make these accusations. Lucio tells the Duke that the friar has spoken against him during his absence. Friar Peter tells the Duke that the friar cannot be summoned because he is ill, and defends him against Lucio's imputations. The Duke appears not to be taking this seriously, asking Angelo, 'Do you not smile at this' (line 163).

Mariana enters, veiled, and is interrogated by the Duke. She admits that she is unmarried but is not a maid: 'I have known my husband, yet my husband / Knows not that ever he knew me' (lines 196–7). Lucio continues to interrupt and is severely reprimanded by the Duke. Mariana names Angelo as her husband and unveils herself, telling the story of the 'bed-trick'. The Duke asks Angelo if this is true. Angelo admits that there was 'some speech of marriage' (line 215) between them but that it was broken off due to Mariana's stained reputation, and he asserts that he has had no contact with her for five years. Angelo tells the Duke that he is the victim of some orchestrated smear by 'some more mightier member' (line 235) than his female accusers, and the Duke gives him authority to punish them, ordering that the friar be sent for. The Duke leaves Angelo to deal with the slanders and makes his exit.

After a few comments from Lucio and Escalus's summoning of Isabella to speak again, the Duke returns in his friar's disguise. Escalus interrogates him and accuses him of slandering Angelo. The disguised Duke describes what he has seen as 'a looker-on here in Vienna' (line 315). Lucio faces the friar and repeats his allegations that he has heard him call the duke 'a fleshmonger, a fool, and a coward' (line 332). There is an altercation as Lucio pulls off the friar's hood to reveal the Duke, who promptly orders Lucio's arrest. The Duke questions Angelo who admits his faults and begs to be put to death. He is ordered to marry Mariana. Turning to Isabella,

> **CONTEXT**
>
> The first printed versions of Shakespeare's plays have relatively few stage directions. Here they indicate that the characters enter 'at several doors' – which may suggest a kind of symbolism as the Duke and his attendants enter from one direction and the remaining characters from another.

the Duke admits that she may wonder why he did not reveal himself sooner and save her brother. Angelo and Mariana are returned, 'new-married' (line 397) and the Duke announces that as requital for the death of Claudio, Angelo must die. Mariana pleads for clemency, and begs Isabella to join in her pleas. She consents and kneels before the Duke, arguing that Angelo's crime was only intended, whereas Claudio deserved his punishment for the enacting of his desires. The Duke hears from the Provost that the order to execute Claudio came privately, and for this disregard of the regulatory procedures, he deprives the Provost of his office. He is sent to bring Barnadine.

Escalus expresses his disappointment that Angelo 'should slip so grossly' (line 469), to which Angelo replies that he craves 'death more willingly than mercy' (line 473). Barnadine and Claudio, his face covered, are brought, as is Juliet.

The Duke pardons Barnadine and bids him live a better life. He then orders that Claudio be uncovered and returns him to Isabella. The Duke asks her to marry him. He announces Angelo's pardon and tells him to 'love your wife' (line 494), and then turns to Lucio. He orders that if there is any woman who has had a child by Lucio, she is to come forward and he will marry her, and then be hanged. Lucio objects, and the Duke moderates the sentence to marriage alone, which Lucio describes as worse than death. 'Slandering a prince deserves it' (line 521) is the Duke's imperious reply. A series of orders – to Claudio to marry Juliet, to Mariana to be happy and to Angelo to love his wife, thanks to Escalus and to the Provost who is promised a better job – ends with the Duke's second proposal to Isabella. She makes no verbal response.

COMMENTARY

This long scene is the culmination of the Duke's plans. All the major characters appear, and are arranged on the stage and dealt their varying punishments. The strain of juggling all the strands of the plot may show at certain points – the Duke cannot think of a good reason why he has to withdraw in order to return as the friar, for example – but he withholds and reveals information with the theatrical delight of a conjuror. Having set up this **dénouement**

> **CONTEXT**
>
> A number of characters – the veiled Mariana, the 'muffled' Claudio, the hooded 'Friar' – are physically uncovered as the visual equivalent of the sequence of revelations in this scene.

where all the main characters will meet, the Duke presides with
evident enjoyment. All his 'actors' play their parts as they have been
told, and the play ends with the marriages characteristic of the finale
of Shakespearean comedy. There are, however, some distinct and
deafening silences. Neither Claudio nor Juliet speaks in the scene,
despite being addressed by the Duke. Angelo makes scant response
to his enforced marriage and to his escape from death. Barnadine
gives no reaction to the unexpected news of his pardon. And most
tellingly of all, Isabella treats the Duke's two offers of marriage with
absolute silence. These silences act as wordless questions, gaps in the
script of the play which can only be filled by our interpretation of
the scene and the whole play. How do these characters react to their
different situations at the end of the play? Shakespeare's conclusion
leaves certain issues unresolved, and it is for the director of the play
in performance to decide, for example, whether Isabella accepts the
Duke's proposal, or whether it looks likely that Angelo will love
Mariana as he is commanded. Optimists might choose to read
silences as a sign of inaudible gratitude; cynics may find them fertile
breeding grounds of dissent at the Duke's interventions. Is his
behaviour justified? Why does he manipulate the disclosure of
information to the last moment? Does he behave justly in his final
apportioning of advice, punishment, and lenity?

'Justice' is a word which echoes through the scene. Isabella, the
Duke, Angelo and Mariana all use it as the play focuses on one of its
key themes in this public arraignment. Through repetition,
however, the word itself and the abstract concept it denotes become
strained, until it is hard to come to any conclusion about what
justice is. Would it be just for Angelo to be killed in punishment for
the death of Claudio? Is it just to suggest that he should be, while
knowing that Claudio is not in fact dead? Is it just to redeem the
irredeemable Barnadine? Is it just to dispense marriage as a
punishment, as the Duke does to both Angelo and Lucio? Should
'slandering a prince' earn whipping? The Duke uses a formulation
which seems to express equivalence and balance, and refers to the
play's title: 'An Angelo for Claudio, death for death' (line 406),
'Like doth quit like, and Measure still for Measure' (line 408) (see
Themes, on **Symmetry and antithesis**).

**CHECK
THE FILM**
The 1978 BBC film
has the Duke hold
out his hand to
Isabella. There is a
pause before she
clasps it, to the
cheers of the
onlookers. They
walk off hand in
hand together,
putting a happy
ending on to the
play's more
ambiguous
conclusion.

CHECK THE BOOK

There are echoes of the biblical story of the 'Sermon on the Mount' in the Duke's language here: look at Matthew 7: 1–7 and Luke 6: 36–42, preferably in the Authorised version of the Bible, rather than a more modern translation.

The image of justice as a balanced set of scales is implicit in this rhetorical arrangement. But the play encourages us to question this apparent neatness, and the justness of such cold legalistic substitutions (see **Themes**, on **Substitution**). It could be argued that the Duke's dispensing of justice represents the ideal of severity tempered with mercy, a Christian ideal, or his desire to see the women beg for Angelo may appear to be a dubious assertion of his legal power (see **Characterisation**).

Isabella's pleas for Angelo demonstrate the extent of her development through the play. As a novice in the convent she was to dedicate her life to God; here she kneels to an earthly ruler for mercy for a condemned man. Her speech rhythms may indicate her unwillingness: a series of monosyllables, a short line at 447, a philosophically and theologically dubious distinction between sinful thoughts and actions. (Isabella contradicts New Testament teaching on the equivalence of intent and action: 'You have heard that it was said by them of old time, Thou shalt not commit adultery: But I say unto you, That whosoever looketh on a woman to lust after her hath committed adultery with her already in his heart' (Matthew 5:27–8).) Elsewhere in the play we have heard her passionate eloquence (II.2, II.4, III.1); by comparison this is forced and unconvincing (see **Characterisation**). Angelo himself is monotone: when the truth is revealed, he wishes only for death. His muted and self-accusing demeanour seems an unsatisfactory basis for marriage, and Mariana's continued faith in him may stretch our credulity. We can only interpret this marriage as a 'happy ending' with a determined suppression of our doubts and misgivings. Lucio's involvement in the scene is as a cheeky commentator, interrupting the solemn proceedings with a stream of one-liners which threaten to steal the limelight from the principals. His treatment may seem particularly harsh, and it is striking that the Duke reserves his harshest words and punishment not for the hypocritical ruler or the convicted murderer but for the man whom he heard slander him. Lucio's transgression in getting Kate Keepdown pregnant serves as a miniature recapitulation of the themes of the play: sex before marriage recalls both Claudio and Angelo, execution for fornication faced also Claudio, and marrying as a punishment with the threat of execution parallels Angelo (see **Themes**, on **Symmetry and antithesis**).

The play's final words are the Duke's promise of revelation: 'So, bring us to our palace, where we'll show / What's yet behind, that's meet you all should know' (lines 535–6). What can he be planning to disclose which has not come to light in this lengthy scene? It is characteristic of the play's tantalising mode that it closes with a hint that we do not, and now never will, know the full story. Effectively, then, the ending is deferred, and it will happen out of our view. Like the Duke himself, the play is effective through managing knowledge and information, and this concluding **couplet** firmly reminds us that there is always more to know.

CONTEXT

The Jacobean playwright Thomas Heywood argued in 1612: 'Tragedies and comedies … differ thus: in comedies, *turbulenta prima, tranquilla ultima*; in tragedies, *tranquilla prima turbulenta ultima*: comedies begin in trouble and end in peace; tragedies begin in calms and end in tempest.'

GLOSSARY

1	cousin courtesy form of address to a fellow nobleman
8	Forerunning more requital preceding other rewards
10	wards of covert bosom the innermost heart
11	characters letters
12	forted fortified
13	razure erasure
20	Vail your regard lower your eyes
30–1	for that … believed if it is not believed I will be punished (for slander)
48	conjure plead
50–1	That thou … madness do not ignore me because you think I am mad
55	characts symbols or badges of rank
	forms ceremonies
66	seems that seems
81	A business for yourself your own business
94	refelled refused
98	concup'sible burning with desire
100	confutes overcomes
107	practice conspiracy
108	it imports no reason it does not make sense
115	ministers angels
130	swinged beaten
131	This' this is
141	touch or soil moral stain continued

142	**ungot** not yet conceived
145	**temporary meddler** one interfering in worldly (temporal) affairs
152	**mere** sole
157	**probation** proof
	make up full clear establish clearly as the truth
158	**convented** summoned
160	**vulgarly** publicly
164	**vanity** futility
179	**punk** prostitute
181	**cause** charge, accusation
197	**all th'effect of love** full sexual intercourse
203	**abuse** deceit
209	**match** appointment
210	**supply thee** satisfy your desires
217	**proportions** dowry
218	**composition** the agreed sum
219	**disvalued** destroyed
230	**confixèd** fastened
233	**touched** wounded
234	**informal** demented
235	**member** person
240	**Compact** conspirator
243	**sealed in approbation** sealed with official endorsement
256–7	**well / Determinèd** made a careful judgement
261	***Cucullus non facit monachum*** (proverbial) the hood does not make the monk
265	**enforce** use, urge
278	**light** randy
290–1	**Respect to … burning throne** I respect your authority, as is even due to the devil for his splendid throne
297	**Good night to your redress** bid farewell to justice
299	**retort** reject
307	**glance** allude
308	**tax him** accuse him
309	**touse** tear

311	hot hasty
314	provincial subject to local laws
330	notedly particularly
331	fleshmonger fornicator
339	close compromise
344	giglots lewd women
351	sheep-biting of the proverbial wolf in sheep's clothing, sneaking, deceitful
	hanged dogs that worried sheep were hanged
361	do thee office be of service to you
367	passes events, trespasses
380	Advertising attentive
	holy dedicated
382	Attorneyed bound
389	rash remonstrance hasty revelation
398	salt lecherous
404	very mercy most merciful aspects
405	proper very
414	mock tantalise
417	imputation accusation, rumour
424	definitive immovable
430	sense reason
432	pavèd bed grave
450	subjects deeds
460	knew it not was not certain
461	advice reflection
469	blood sexual appetite
479	squar'st conducts
480	quit remit, pardon
493	quits requites
495	apt remission willing forgiveness
498	luxury lechery
517	Remit thy other forfeits cancel your other punishments
519	pressing to death form of torture in which the prisoner was pressed with heavy weights until he pleaded or died continued

CONTEXT

From 'forfeits in a barber's shop' (line 319) it seems that barbers had lists of mock-penalties for misbehaviour by customers, but since barbers also acted as surgeons and dentists, their forfeits, or items set up as an example to others, might be more grisly.

> 526   **more behind** more to follow
>
>   **gratulate** pleasing
>
> 532   **motion** proposal
>
>   **imports your good** will bring you great benefit

EXTENDED COMMENTARIES

TEXT 1 (I.3.19–54)

CONTEXT

The images of disorder in the Duke's speech refer to doctrines of social stability, sometimes called the 'Elizabethan World Picture' following an influential exposition by E. M. W. Tillyard in 1943.

DUKE: We have strict statutes and most biting laws,
The needful bits and curbs to headstrong weeds,   20
Which for this fourteen years we have let slip;
Even like an o'ergrown lion in a cave,
That goes not out to prey. Now, as fond fathers,
Having bound up the threatening twigs of birch,
Only to stick it in their children's sight
For terror, not to use, in time the rod
Becomes more mocked than feared, so our decrees,
Dead to infliction, to themselves are dead,
And liberty plucks justice by the nose;
The baby beats the nurse, and quite athwart   30
Goes all decorum.
FRIAR THOMAS: It rested in your grace
To unloose this tied-up justice when you pleased,
And it in you more dreadful would have seemed
Than in Lord Angelo.
DUKE: I do fear, too dreadful.
Sith 'twas my fault to give the people scope,
'Twould be my tyranny to strike and gall them
For what I bid them do: for we bid this be done
When evil deeds have their permissive pass
And not the punishment. Therefore, indeed, my father,
I have on Angelo imposed the office,   40
Who may, in th'ambush of my name, strike home,
And yet my nature never in the sight
To do it slander. And to behold his sway
I will, as 'twere a brother of your order,

Visit both prince and people. Therefore, I prithee,
Supply me with the habit, and instruct
How I may formally in person bear me
Like a true friar. More reasons for this action
At our more leisure shall I render you;
Only this one – Lord Angelo is precise,   50
Stands at a guard with envy, scarce confesses
That his blood flows, or that his appetite
Is more to bread than stone. Hence shall we see,
If power change purpose, what our seemers be.
>   *Exeunt*

This scene gives some further information about the Duke's
character and motives in giving up his authority to Angelo,
following on from the previous scene in which Claudio is arrested, a
casualty of Angelo's new regime. In I.2, first Lucio and his friends
and then Claudio discuss the Duke's absence: here, in conversation
with Friar Thomas, the Duke appears to talk about the state of
Vienna and the collapse of discipline and respect for the law.

The Duke paints a picture of the world turned upside down because
the laws have not been enforced: 'quite athwart / Goes all decorum'
(lines 30–1). He uses a sequence of animal and social imagery to
convey this disturbed state, and his first image is a mixed **metaphor**
which may highlight both the topsy-turvy state of Vienna and of the
Duke himself. Line 20's 'bits and curbs to headstrong weeds' begins
with the imagery of riding and controlling a horse and turns to the
image of the unweeded garden as a symbol of political disorder. The
law has been like an 'o-ergrown lion in a cave' (line 22) which does
not go out hunting, and the **simile** aptly conveys the picture of a
once terrible and lordly beast run to fat and indolence. The image of
the baby beating the nurse (line 30) makes another comparison with
an unnatural situation as an indication of how out of order matters
have got – instead of receiving correction from its nurse, the infant
itself dispenses punishment. Through the language of his speech of
lines 19–31, the Duke stresses the irregularity of social affairs
because of the breakdown of law and order. His word 'terror' (line
26) echoes his use at I.1.19, in which the Duke seems to identify
'terror' as the prerogative of authority. Indeed, the Duke's language

> **CONTEXT**
>
> Compare the
> Duke's imagery
> here with
> Claudio's
> description of
> Angelo's
> governorship as
> that of a man on a
> new mount
> showing the beast
> who is in control
> in the previous
> scene (I.2.158ff).

is full of violence: the lawless state he represents is a hostile and
dangerous one, but then so is the law itself. His view of the law here
is as a punitive instrument of corporal punishment, which contrasts
with his apparent embrace of the concept of mercy in the final
scene. The law ought to be 'biting' (line 19); 'threatening twigs of
birch' wielded by fathers against their children; the rod ought to be
'feared' (line 27); the baby 'beats' the nurse (line 30); it would 'be
my tyranny to strike and gall them' (line 36); Angelo 'may, in
th'ambush of my name, strike home' (line 41).

Throughout his first speech, the Duke's imagery distances him from
the events he describes. The use of the pronoun 'we' (line 19)
suggests only a formal responsibility for what is happening: this is
the 'we' of the public figure, the representative of the state and the
law. Friar Thomas' intervention, however, switches the
responsibility for the law on to the Duke personally. His mild but
inescapable question asks why the Duke did not use his authority
'to unloose this tied-up justice' (line 32), and the image suggests
disorder since here it is justice which is imprisoned rather than
doing the imprisoning. The Duke's response is immediately in the
first person: 'I do fear …' (line 34), followed by a sequence of
similar pronouns in the next three lines. It is the nearest he comes to
an admission of liability for the state the law is in: 'twas my fault to
give the people scope' (line 35). The word 'scope', as well as the
friar's suggestion that the law should be released, recalls the
recurrent theme of liberty and restraint running throughout the
play (see **Themes**). The Duke seems to draw back from his
acknowledgement, however, and resume his formal, public pronoun
'for we bid this be done' (line 37), although the rest of the speech is
peppered with the first-person pronouns. It could be argued that
part of reason for the Duke's withdrawal from his office is
psychological, and that here he is taking a first step towards freeing
himself from his public role in order to investigate and develop a
private self, a man who can say 'I' rather than a ruler who always
declares 'we' (see **Characterisation**).

In this scene, Friar Thomas serves only as a pretext for the Duke's
self-revelation. He does not appear anywhere else in the play, and
when the Duke needs a trustworthy friar later on, one Friar Peter is

**CHECK
THE BOOK**

In John Sutherland's
collection of essays
*Henry V, War
Criminal?* (2000) he
asks 'Why does the
Duke leave?' – and
concludes: 'the
Duke leaves Vienna
because it no longer
needs Dukes'.

found. He does, however, provide the Duke with the disguise from which he can view his subjects and his deputy during the play. The Duke asks him for the habit and for some instruction, although it seems clear that this is to be an assumed role rather than a religious vocation. The audience is let into this secret: whereas all the other characters are taken in by the disguise (although some productions and some critics argue that Lucio sees through it), the audience always has this superior knowledge. The Duke promises more reasons for his actions later on, but delivers one important clue in the last lines of the scene. His thoughts shift to Angelo, and to his outward appearances and declarations. 'Hence we shall see, / If power change purpose, what our seemers be' (lines 53–4): the end-rhyme and the positioning of these lines at the end of a scene both add emphasis to this pronouncement, which suggests that the Duke's primary purpose is to test his suspicions about Angelo's virtue and honour. The Duke, it seems, has a plan even at this early stage of the play, and the scene invites us – 'hence we shall see' – to watch the spectacle unfold and act as witnesses to this extended and hidden trial. In its suggestion of a possible gap between 'seeming' and 'being', it is a hint of what is to come, giving the Duke an aura of control and foresight as he dons his monk's robe and cowl.

TEXT 2 (II.2.28–82)

ISABELLA: Please but your honour hear me.
ANGELO: Well, what's your suit?
ISABELLA: There is a vice that most I do abhor,
And most desire should meet the blow of justice,   30
For which I would not plead, but that I must,
For which I must not plead, but that I am
At war 'twixt will and will not.
ANGELO: Well: the matter?
ISABELLA: I have a brother is condemned to die.
I do beseech you, let it be his fault,
And not my brother.
PROVOST: (*aside*)   Heaven give thee moving graces.
ANGELO: Condemn the fault, and not the actor of it?
Why, every fault's condemned ere it be done.
Mine were the very cipher of a function,

CONTEXT

George Whetstone's *Promos and Cassandra*, one of Shakespeare's sources for the play, takes its title from its two central protagonists – the equivalents of *Measure for Measure*'s Angelo and Isabella – giving them and the relationship between them centre stage, as in this scene.

To fine the faults whose fine stands in record, 40
And let go by the actor.
ISABELLA: O just, but severe law!
I had a brother then; heaven keep your honour.
LUCIO: (*aside to* Isabella) Give't not o'er so. To him again, entreat him,
Kneel down before him, hang upon his gown;
You are too cold. If you should need a pin,
You could not with more tame a tongue desire it.
To him, I say.
ISABELLA: Must he needs die?
ANGELO: Maiden, no remedy.
ISABELLA: Yes, I do think that you might pardon him,
And neither heaven nor man grieve at the mercy. 50
ANGELO: I will not do't.
ISABELLA: But can you if you would?
ANGELO: Look what I will not, that I cannot do.
ISABELLA But might you do't, and do the world no wrong,
If so your heart were touched with that remorse
As mine is to him?
ANGELO: He's sentenced; 'tis too late.
LUCIO: (*aside to* Isabella) You are too cold.
ISABELLA: Too late? Why, no. I that do speak a word
May call it back again. Well, believe this,
No ceremony that to great ones longs,
Not the king's crown, nor the deputed sword, 60
The marshal's truncheon, nor the judge's robe,
Become them with one half so good a grace
As mercy does.
If he had been as you, and you, as he,
You would have slipped like him; but he, like you,
Would not have been so stern.
ANGELO: Pray you, be gone.
ISABELLA: I would to heaven I had your potency,
And you were Isabel; should it then be thus?
No, I would tell what 'twere to be a judge,
And what a prisoner.
LUCIO: (*aside to* Isabella) Ay, touch him; there's the vein. 70
ANGELO: Your brother is a forfeit of the law,

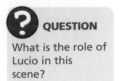

QUESTION

What is the role of Lucio in this scene?

And you but waste your words.
ISABELLA: Alas, alas;
Why, all the souls that were were forfeit once,
And He that might the vantage best have took
Found out the remedy. How would you be,
If He, which is the top of judgement, should
But judge you as you are? O think on that,
And mercy then will breathe within your lips,
Like man new made.
ANGELO: Be you content, fair maid,
It is the law, not I, condemns your brother;   80
Were he my kinsman, brother, or my son,
It should be thus with him. He must die tomorrow.

This first meeting between Angelo and Isabella is remarkable for its
use of language and rhythm to convey the intensity of the
relationship which is so quickly forged between the two
protagonists.

Something of the dynamic between Angelo and Isabella can be
discerned simply by looking at the shape of the scene on the printed
page, and in particular at the pattern of lines in which the metre,
almost like the baton in a relay race, swaps between two speakers.
Isabella's first two speeches leave a gap in which Angelo inserts a
terse question. It is almost as if the incomplete pentameter forces
Angelo to reply, leaving a measurable silence in the metre of the line
which he has to fill up. Later in the scene the roles are reversed as
Isabella completes Angelo's lines. When he says 'I will not do't'
(line 51), the position of the words in the pentameter undermines
their stated meaning: while the words themselves speak of certainty
and finality, the rhythm is half-finished, leaving a space in which
Isabella can – metrically must – reopen the argument. The metrical
space serves to prolong the interview: although Angelo's words say
that there is no room for argument over Claudio's sentence, he does
not, at some level, want to dismiss her entirely. At one point he tries
to evade the logic of the completed pentameter, following her half-
line 'As mine is to him?' (line 55) by assertively beginning a new
line: 'He's sentenced' (line 56). At another point she seems to expect
some reply to her incomplete line 'As mercy does' (line 63), and

CONTEXT

A freer use of the
blank verse line, as
here in this scene,
is often seen as a
sign of
Shakespeare's
increasing poetic
flexibility as his
career progresses.
Certainly his
earlier plays tend
to have more
complete and end-
stopped verse
lines, and a higher
proportion of
rhyme, than his
later ones where
prose and a more
elastic use of
blank verse tend
to dominate.

CHECK THE BOOK

Books by voice coaches aimed at actors often have great insights into the energy of Shakespeare's verse. Have a look at Cicely Berry, *The Actor and His Text*, (1987), or Patsy Rodenburg's *Speaking Shakespeare* (2002).

when no intervention from Angelo is forthcoming, she has to take a deep breath and start another phrase. The battle between them is thus conducted through control of the language and metre of their altercation, and the ways in which their language comes together to form the pentameters of **blank verse** suggests a definite relationship between them.

The language of this extract therefore demonstrates the extent to which each is intensely aware of the other. They are circling round each other, almost dancing, locked together in the rhythms of argument and debate. Lucio's persistent injunctions to her to warm up are never directly answered or acknowledged: the pair hardly seem to notice his presence, or that of the Provost. Perhaps it is no wonder that Angelo finds the encounter so stimulating, as he reveals in his **soliloquy** at the end of the scene: the back-and-forth of their exchange has a kind of sensuous energy. Juliet Stevenson, who played Isabella at the RSC in 1983, has described the language in this scene as 'erotic', suggesting '[Isabella] and Angelo have been copulating across the verse ever since they met' (see **Critical history**). How far Isabella is aware of this sexual current is a question for performance (see **Characterisation**).

As well as the erotics of the encounter, this scene dramatises some of the extremes of the play's ethical framework. At first, Angelo tries to hide behind a formal, impersonal concept of the law. He replies to 'Must he needs die?' with the bland 'Maiden, no remedy' (line 48), but Isabella wrong-foots him into taking responsibility for the decision. By introducing the insistent first-person: 'I do think that you might pardon him', Isabella puts the onus on Angelo, the man standing before her, rather than on some abstracted and intangible legal function, and he responds: 'I will not do't' (line 51). It is an unwilling concession by which Angelo acknowledges that he is personally responsible, and Isabella uses this as a weakened point in his resistance, seizing on the possibility of working a further concession. Her prime weapon is the emotive figure of substitution (see **Themes**, on **Substitution**): she repeatedly invites, even demands, that Angelo see the situation from different viewpoints, that he imagine himself in a different role: 'If he had been as you, and you as he' (line 64); 'I would to heaven I had your potency, /

And you were Isabel' (lines 67–8); 'How would you be, / If He, which is the top of judgement, should / But judge you as you are?' (lines 75–7). Angelo tries to reinstate some distance between his private person and his public position: 'It is the law, not I, condemns your brother' (line 80): like the Duke in I.3 (see **Text 1**), he is hesitant around his personal responsibility, preferring to present the law as separate and autonomous.

Isabella also works on Angelo by taking up his words and giving them new meanings. She turns his terms of earthly justice, that Claudio 'is a forfeit of the law' (line 71), and ups the moral stakes by transforming them into spiritual ones: 'all the souls that were were forfeit once' (line 73), so that the repetition of the word makes Claudio and Angelo equal with all the rest of sinful humanity. She presents the case for mercy as the prerequisite of the great ruler. After a shaky start – her 'let it be his fault, / And not my brother' (lines 35–6) is awkwardly phrased, and it seems that Angelo will be able to brush her off without difficulty. His rhetorical question (line 37) exposes the weakness of her opening salvo, and she is ready to give up. Urged on by Lucio, however, her arguments gain in eloquence and passion: Angelo has relatively little to say for himself in this early part of their encounter. What is clear, however, is the erotic and philosophic concentration of their meeting, as the scene continues to dramatise a relationship which creates a palpable electric energy.

TEXT 3 (III.1.57–88)

CLAUDIO: Now, sister, what's the comfort?
ISABELLA: Why,
As all comforts are: most good, most good indeed.
Lord Angelo, having affairs to heaven,   60
Intends you for his swift ambassador,
Where you shall be an everlasting leiger.
Therefore your best appointment make with speed;
Tomorrow you set on.
CLAUDIO: Is there no remedy?
ISABELLA: None, but such remedy as, to save a head,
To cleave a heart in twain.
CLAUDIO: But is there any?

CHECK THE NET

Check out a great collection of critical essays, reviews of productions and other resources at **www.holycross. edu/departments/ theatre/projects/ isp/measure/ mainmenu.html**.

ISABELLA: Yes, brother, you may live;
There is a devilish mercy in the judge,
If you'll implore it, that will free your life,
But fetter you till death.   70
CLAUDIO: Perpetual durance?
ISABELLA: Ay, just. Perpetual durance, a restraint,
Though all the world's vastidity you had,
To a determined scope.
CLAUDIO: But in what nature?
ISABELLA: In such a one as, you consenting to't,
Would bark your honour from that trunk you bear,
And leave you naked.
CLAUDIO: Let me know the point.
ISABELLA: O, I do fear thee, Claudio, and I quake
Lest thou a feverous life shouldst entertain,
And six or seven winters more respect
Than a perpetual honour. Dar'st thou die?   80
The sense of death is most in apprehension,
And the poor beetle that we tread upon
In corporal sufferance finds a pang as great
As when a giant dies.
CLAUDIO: Why give you me this shame?
Think you I can a resolution fetch
From flowery tenderness? If I must die,
I will encounter darkness as a bride,
And hug it in mine arms.

> **CONTEXT**
>
> Perhaps
> Shakespeare's
> most famous
> brother and sister
> are Laertes and
> Ophelia (*Hamlet*).
> Generally he
> prefers to explore
> other types of
> family
> relationships –
> fathers and
> daughters, twins,
> mothers and sons.

When Claudio was arrested in Act I, his sister Isabella occurs to him as the only possibility of helping his situation. He tells Lucio that he has 'great hope' (I.2.181) in her powers of persuading Angelo, and Lucio replies 'I pray she may' (line 186). Isabella herself is confident that she will succeed, sending Lucio with a message back to Claudio, promising 'Soon at night / I'll send him certain word of my success' (I.4.89). When she has refused Angelo's sexual bargain, she assures herself in her only **soliloquy** that Claudio would rather die twenty times over than suffer her to experience 'such abhorred pollution' (II.4.183). She will break the news to him and 'fit his mind for death, for his soul's rest' (II.4.188). All this, plus Claudio's own interview with the disguised Duke and his resignation around

death at the beginning of III.1, serves to build up the tension around
the first meeting of brother and sister: this is the scene when she has
to confess her failure – some might call it her unwillingness – to save
him. How will each respond to the other?

The Duke and the Provost withdraw: Claudio is eager for news,
'what's the comfort?' (III.1.57). Despite his expressed readiness for
death after the Duke's long homily (III.1.5ff), he is clearly desperate
for an escape. Isabella's 'Well' (line 58) is a word alone on a line. It is
possible to imagine her steeling herself in that pause, taking a deep
breath, to tell her unwelcome news, and this long hesitation created
by the lineation may also suggest that she is not quite so sure of
Claudio's reactions as she professed herself at the end of II.4. She
uses a technique identifiable in her interview with Angelo in the
previous scene (see **Text 2**): picking up 'comfort' (line 57), to which
Claudio gives an immediate, earthly meaning, and transforming it
into the religious idea of comfort in heaven after death. Claudio
takes 'Perpetual durance' (line 70) to mean the commutation of his
sentence from execution to life imprisonment; for Isabella the words
mean the eternal imprisonment of the sinful soul or the stained
conscience. It is noticeable that whereas the Duke's speech on death
was entirely without an idea of Christian salvation, Isabella's view
of death is entirely conditioned by her religious convictions. Death
for her is therefore a very different prospect.

QUESTION

How does
Isabella's vocation
as a nun make
itself felt in her
speech and actions
during the play?

Isabella's delivery of her news is circumlocutory: she uses the image
of Claudio as an ambassador going to heaven as if it were another
court, preparing the way for his ruler. His 'Is there no remedy?'
(line 64) precisely echoes Angelo's 'no remedy' at II.2.48, and he
breaks in on Isabella's religious approach to his fate with an urgent
question. This desperate questioning recurs at lines 66, 70, 73 and
84: Claudio is unable to accept the finality of his fate, perhaps
because Isabella admits that there is, in fact, a remedy, albeit one
that would 'cleave a heart in twain' (line 66). Her obfuscation,
perhaps born of fear about his reaction, gives him space to hope,
and he worries away at her more poetic, obscure diction with terse
interrogatives. This space for hope is literally present in her
unfinished pentameters, which leave a metrical gap for him to fill
(see also **Text 2**). She is able to interpret his response: 'I do fear thee'

(line 77). Isabella's language is full of rather formal words: Shakespeare does not use 'leiger' (line 62) or 'vastidity' (line 72) anywhere else, and 'durance' (line 70) is also a rarity. These unfamiliar, carefully chosen words convey a kind of stiffness, even coldness, about Isabella, as if they are from a speech she has prepared (compare Angelo's 'prolixious' at II.4.162, or Isabella's 'promprure' at II.4.178, neither of which occurs anywhere else in Shakespeare). Claudio castigates her use of language: 'Think you I can a resolution fetch / From flowery tenderness?' (lines 85–6). Only action, not talk, can ameliorate the situation.

At the centre of the play, III.1 is a scene of contrasting philosophies and emotions, from Claudio's stoicism to his desperate fear of death, from Isabella's tentative explanation to her anger and hurt, from the 'friar's' long speech on the worthlessness of life to the Duke's prose plottings and intrigues. This extract contains, on a smaller scale, something of the same conflict. Isabella's language is focused on heaven and on the spirituality of eternal life; Claudio's is on the immediacy of his predicament. She balances life against death, a 'head' against a 'heart' (lines 65–6), freedom against fetters (lines 69–70), 'restraint' against 'scope' (lines 71–3). Isabella's attempts at comfort are sometimes unwittingly tactless: the image of the beetle's suffering in death compared to a giant's (lines 82–4) seems to stress rather than diminish 'corporal sufferance' (line 83) through comparison. Isabella's argument rests on her perspective that there is 'a fate worse than death' – a tainted and sinful life; for Claudio the imminence of his execution means that his concerns are more earthly and physical. Even his imagery of death is sexualised, made physical. He is not comforted by her vision of heavenly consolation, rather he sees 'darkness as a bride' he will 'hug' (lines 83–4) to himself. This imagery links his fate to its cause, his crime of fornication. Claudio's responses to Isabella's disclosure about her dealings with Angelo prepare the audience for his pleas with his sister later in the scene.

CONTEXT

Shakespeare is often credited with introducing new words to the English language, or at least being the first person to write them down. He has been estimated to have a vocabulary of around 30,000 words.

PART THREE

CRITICAL APPROACHES

CHARACTERISATION

Characters in a play are just that: characters. It may seem obvious to say that they are not real people and that they should not be discussed as such. They consist of what they say and what is said about them: they are composed of words, not of flesh and blood, nor of inner psychology. It is significant that the very word 'character' derives from words denoting marking or writing (as in its uses in *Measure for Measure*, for example at V.1.11), only gaining its modern meanings of 'individual personality' or 'person in a play' in the late seventeenth century. Sometimes Shakespearean characters have a representative, rather than an individual, function: they embody behaviours or conditions as symbolic **personifications**. Sometimes naming can be a clue to this: the names 'Angelo', for example, or even 'Abhorson', have clear symbolic connotations (whereas the name 'Isabella' does not). Some characters exist as dramatic devices rather than as fully realised individuals. It is difficult to deduce much about Mariana except, perhaps, that there is nothing to deduce about her beyond her role in the Duke's scheme. Similarly, Barnadine is an irrelevant character in plot terms – it would be much more streamlined to have Ragozine's fortuitous death as the answer to Angelo's demand for the head of Claudio (see **Themes**, on **Substitution**) than to introduce an intermediate character. The reasons for Barnadine's presence in the play, therefore, may be seen as more symbolic: he represents an unregenerate and extreme form of immorality and thus his pardon at the end of the play needs to be examined alongside those of the others.

At other points Shakespeare's gift for recognisable and distinctive characterisation is evident: single phrases or gestures can suggest an entire personality. In performance the assumptions of the **Method** school tend to dominate, whereby the inner motivations of the characters – their life beyond what is written for them in the play – are a crucial part of directors' and actors' interpretation. These notes on characters use information from performances where it offers a

> **CONTEXT**
>
> Method Acting is a technique of acting based on the theories of Russian actor and director Konstantin Stanislavsky (1863–1938) in which ideas about the inner motivations and psychology of a character are the basis of the performance.

particular slant, but they also try to remember that Shakespeare's characters derive from an age in which personality and the sense of the individual were quite different from now, and especially that they are part of a theatrical culture in which **verisimilitude** is not always the prime concern. Shakespeare's concern with balance and symmetry in this play (see **Themes**, on **Symmetry and antithesis**) also means that characters should not only be analysed as distinct individuals but also in different combinations and comparisons. Characterisation forms part of the overall structure of the play, and should not be considered in isolation from its themes and language.

THE DUKE

CHECK THE BOOK

Look at different interpretations of the Duke's character by Wilson Knight in the *Casebook* on the play (ed. C. K. Stead, 1971) and by Richard Wilson in Nigel Wood (ed.), *Measure for Measure* (1996).

How the Duke's character is interpreted has a crucial effect on the interpretation of the whole play. Is he, as Lucio avers, a 'Duke of dark corners' (IV.3.156) or does he bear 'the sword of heaven' (III.2.249)? Is his 'ethical attitude exactly correspondent with Jesus', as the critic G. Wilson Knight has suggested, or is he a Machiavellian powermonger who moves unseen and all-seeing among his people in order better to dominate them, as has been argued by Richard Wilson? (See **Critical history**). These interpretations locate the Duke in two different plays. A Christ-like Duke brings about a redemptive happy ending; a political manipulator is out for himself. As these Notes have attempted to argue throughout, the interest of the questions and problems thrown up by *Measure for Measure* lies in their possibilities rather than decisive interpretations: what is interesting and significant about the characterisation of the Duke is that it can sustain such diverse readings.

The Duke's first appearance in I.1 is mysterious. Why is he leaving and why does he promote the untested Angelo? His speeches are lengthy and reflective, turning to the philosophical, and sometimes difficult to penetrate. They are not the direct and purposeful instructions of an efficient ruler making preparations for an unavoidable absence. Perhaps the **syntax** represents mental unease: the breakdown of order in the state may be reflected, or may itself reflect a breakdown in the Duke. (The physical and moral health of the nation and of its ruler were often allied in Renaissance political philosophy.) There are suggestions that he longs for solitude as he declines any ceremony on his departure: 'I love the people, / But do not like to stage me to their eyes' (I.1.67–8). This is a repeated theme of the Duke's character: he tells Friar Thomas in I.3 that he has 'ever loved the life removed' (line 8), and in IV.1, while Isabella discusses his plan with Mariana, the Duke soliloquises, apparently unprompted, on the 'millions of false eyes' which are stuck on 'place and greatness' (line 59). Perhaps the Duke's adoption of a disguise by which he can move about, seeing but unseen, hidden from view by the cowl of his habit, is his attempt to redress the disadvantage of his public role. Instead of being a spectacle to be looked at, his is the seeing eye. Like a mirror he turns back the looks of those who would look at him and makes them look at themselves. This may have sinister implications: many recent critics have discussed the Duke's preoccupation with covert surveillance of his population as a form of tyrannical power (see **Critical history**), or it may be seen to enforce the associations of the Duke with an omniscient, all-seeing divinity.

As with so much of his behaviour, the Duke's motives for abdicating his office are opaque. Lucio boasts 'I believe I know the cause of his withdrawing' (III.2.125), but then keeps the suspense ''Tis a secret must be locked within the teeth and lips' (line 128). The play seems to acknowledge the gap in explanation for this crucial step: in the first act the Duke promises further elaboration 'at our more leisure' (I.3.49), and at the play's conclusion he is still harping on the story yet to be told: 'So bring us to our palace, where we'll show / What's yet behind, that's meet you all should know' (V.1.536). The Duke tells Friar Thomas that it is not love which prompts his actions. His description of a 'complete bosom' (line 3) suggests an emotional self-sufficiency, which he echoes in his disguise as the friar in the face of Lucio's accusations, claiming that the Duke was 'not inclined' (III.2.116) towards sexual activity. His treatment of Lucio, however, seems to suggest that he is not as 'complete' as he might like to be, and that he is affected by other people's opinions. He seeks reassurance from Escalus after Lucio's tirade. The Duke tells Friar Thomas that he has a 'purpose / More grave and wrinkled than the aims and ends / Of burning youth' (I.3.5–6) (although his view of a happy ending for himself seems to include marriage to Isabella), and he goes on to suggest three reasons, including the desire for seclusion, for his retirement from

CONTEXT

Critics have seen the Duke as a figure for Christ and for King James I.

CONTEXT

There are friars elsewhere in Shakespeare's work, in *Romeo and Juliet* and in *Much Ado About Nothing*. Although Shakespearean England was mistrustful of friars as representatives of Catholicism, Shakespeare tends to view them more sympathetically in his plays.

office. He discusses the way the law has fallen into disuse, and argues that, having presided over its decline, he cannot justly reinforce it, and he also suggests that he wants to test Angelo and see 'if power change purpose, what our seemers be' (I.3.54). This last reason may hint at a more manipulative, Machiavellian, side to his character and a cavalier attitude to the casualties of Angelo's regime. If he already suspects Angelo, it is surely ethically questionable to allow him the power to abuse the Viennese populace. If the whole play is set up as a test for Angelo, however, its other characters are also subjected to testing, even the Duke himself. Roger Allam, who played the Duke for the Royal Shakespeare Company in 1987, felt that he 'constantly uses other people, Angelo, Claudio, Isabella, even Lucio, as a means of self-knowledge': through them he gains understanding of himself.

The idea that the Duke is on a quest for self-knowledge is commonly asserted. For Daniel Massey, another RSC Duke (in 1983), 'a gesture as immense as handing over the reins of power to a young and relatively inexperienced Angelo must go hand in hand, I felt, with some sort of psychological crisis. Perhaps it is an act of desperation. In any event, I divined … a passionate desire to put things right.' Roger Allam agreed with this line of interpretation, arguing that his character 'seemed to be in the midst of a deep personal crisis about the value of life itself'. The sense of paralysis brought on by this philosophical and psychological dilemma was indicated in this production's presentation of the opening scene, where the Duke sat 'transfixed, staring into space, while around him civil servants were trying to get him to sign important papers'. Both these Dukes, then, leave their office to pursue some personal goal, to set off on a journey of self-discovery through and during which they work out their roles and responsibilities. The play certainly sustains this interpretation – indeed, when he is quizzed by the 'friar', Escalus's first description of the Duke is as 'One that, above all other strifes, contended especially to know himself' (III.2.222–3) – but it also allows for a Duke who is politically calculating and cold-blooded rather than psychologically bruised and reflective.

In the early part of the play, the Duke is concerned with abdication, with giving up his powers and with a retreat into a less active life.

As the truth about Angelo's behaviour emerges, however, he becomes more and more active, spinning his complicated plans to bring about the resolution. Whereas the first half of the play could be seen to derive its energy from the encounters between Angelo and Isabella, the second half is dominated, prompted, by the Duke. His new-found activity is analogous to that of the dramatic author or director: he invents a plot and positions his characters, while enjoying superior knowledge about how events will turn out. This firmness of purpose involves a certain amount of cruelty to the participants. The Duke could have revealed himself to countermand the order to execute Claudio, but instead he delivers a long homily on life's empty pleasures and bids the hapless prisoner 'Be absolute for death' (III.1.5). He could have told Isabella that Claudio had in fact been spared, but instead his announcement that her brother is dead is abrupt and callous. He makes Mariana think that her long-awaited husband is to be executed and puts Isabella to the humiliation of begging for the life of a man at whose hands she has suffered. He even lets the Provost think he has lost his job for disobeying orders. In the last scene the other characters on stage seem puppets in the Duke's hands and only Lucio, in his audacious unmasking of the 'friar', offers a challenge to this tyranny, exercised through a combination of plotting and quick improvisation. For Roger Allam as the Duke, this last scene 'felt as if I was subjecting them, Isabella, Angelo, and Mariana, to some kind of ordeal by fire. The sequence as a whole had the ritual of purification.' Another more cynical reading might suggest that it registers the Duke's resumption of office, his sense of, and renewed enjoyment in, his own autocratic power. It is a power before which Lucio's unwitting crime of 'Slandering a prince' (V.1.521) is one of the worst of all offences.

ISABELLA

Isabella is a character who seems to demand us to understand her better than she understands herself. Her decision to enter a convent is never explained, and many critics have sought to characterise this as a running away, a desire to escape the problems and pressures of 'real life', rather than as a considered consequence of her piety. A widespread assumption that the nun's vow of chastity means that

> **CONTEXT**
>
> In Shakespeare's theatre, Isabella, like the other female characters, would have been played by a young male actor, since women were not allowed to appear on stage.

she is sexually repressed, a hotbed of seething and barely restrained passions, has affected interpretations of Isabella's character. Certainly, Isabella is not unaffected by her involvement in a plot which is preoccupied by illicit sexuality. She is the focus of the play's sexual dynamic, as Angelo finds himself almost overwhelmed with desire, and even the Duke proposes marriage to her. She is implicated in the play's grubby sex plot, and without a qualm she engineers the bed-trick, subjecting another woman to the sexual fate she so vehemently defends herself against. Some critics have read in her language a subconscious eroticism, notably in her sensuous desire 'to strip myself to death as to a bed / That long I have been sick for' (II.4.102–3) rather than submit to Angelo. Paola Dionisotti, who played Isabella for the RSC in 1978, described her character as 'innocent, not naïve' – she is, after all, able to play the grubby game of blackmail with Angelo when she threatens 'Sign me a present pardon for my brother, / Or with an outstretched throat I'll tell the world / What man thou art' (II.4.152–4). The 1978 production used Isabella's costume to suggest 'her increasing ambivalence towards retreat' through the alterations to her habit : 'the hood came back, the sleeves got rolled up, dirt appeared at the hem'. Dionisotti added that 'my Isabella was very frightened of sexuality … [she] doesn't particularly enjoy being among people … because people are so complicated to deal with, and you have to deal with all their contradiction, and of course their contradictions force you to look at your own, which is what Claudio does to Isabella. Isabella craves simplicity and order and certainty – her belief – but is faced with confusion and contradiction – humanity.' For another Isabella, Juliet Stevenson, who took on the role in 1983, Isabella was a much more positive character, one who 'recognises her own sensuality and the need to apply strict control over it. I don't think she's frightened or surprised by it; she wants to dominate it.' This recalls Isabella's request for 'more stricter restraint' (I.4.4) in her earliest words in the play. Both these actors' interpretations stress Isabella's need for control – of herself or of her environment – and this element of her character connects with Angelo's similar need for restraint, of himself and others.

It is in her two scenes opposite Angelo, and one with her brother, that Isabella's character expresses its energy. The play offers her

QUESTION

Why doesn't Isabella return to the convent at the end of the play?

little room for **soliloquy**: hers is a character which emerges through her interaction with others. Her only moment alone on stage is her short speech after her interview with Angelo at the end of II.4, in which she acknowledges her own isolation: 'To whom should I complain?' (II.4.171). It is at this point that she delivers the line which is perhaps most difficult for modern readers and audiences to accept, 'More than our brother is our chastity' (II.4.185). Even here, she avoids the direct, confessional first-person form of address – it is not 'more than *my* brother is *my* chastity'. This is a formal statement of belief rather than an inner revelation of feeling. Unlike Angelo, she does not seem to struggle with her conscience, but instead comes to an adamant, even extreme, certainty which many readers have found unsympathetic. But in a more religious age, life itself seemed a short and insignificant matter in the light of eternal judgement. 'Death is a fearful thing' – perhaps Claudio's terror speaks more immediately to us now, but Isabella's reply 'And shamèd life a hateful' (III.1.120–1) represents the moral orthodoxy of the time, and no one in the play itself criticises her for this firm belief, as even Claudio repents of his attempts to persuade her otherwise. It is striking that the most fervent (or is it ironic?) appreciation of her piety comes from the irreverent Lucio, who describes her as 'a thing enskied and ensainted' (I.4.34). Her declarations of her faith, as for example, at II.2.73ff, sound a note of real conviction, particularly when compared to the sententious wisdom of the Duke (III.1.5ff). He is always a fake friar, whereas her calling is a genuine one.

Isabella's character blossoms in debate. At first she is hesitant and timorous with Angelo, but on Lucio's insistence she reveals her determined and expressive nature. Claudio's description of her 'prosperous art / When she will play with reason and discourse, / And well she can persuade' (I.2.183–5) is amply realised in the presentation of her arguments to his judge. After the emotional roller-coaster of the first scene in Act III, however, her role is less prominent – she appears tired and compliant in place of her fierce and eloquent passions in the first half of the play. Her weariness seems almost palpable by the final scene: she expresses no welcome or relief at Claudio's deliverance, and her plea for Angelo's remission is stilted and forced, particularly by contrast to her

> **CONTEXT**
>
> When Judi Dench played the role of Isabella in 1962, she spoke the troublesome line 'more than our brother is our chastity' 'in an agonized whisper, as if appalled that the truth should be so hard'. See Robert Speaight, *Shakespeare on the Stage* (1973).

QUESTION

Ruthless puritan or
saintly heroine?
What is your view
of Isabella?

heartfelt petition for her brother's life. In her first appearance she is
taken from the convent to which she wants to dedicate her life, and
she never returns there. Her response to the Duke's proposal is
enigmatically silent, and this is perhaps the logical conclusion of her
increasingly muted presence throughout the play. Does she marry
him or not? The play allows us to decide. Her silence may be
interpreted as a sign of resistance to his plans, or as wordless
compliance. And either of these alternatives begs further questions.
Would she reject the Duke because she is repressed or frightened, as
an agony aunt might put it, of commitment? Or because she is
committed to her religious vocation and has no need of a husband?
Or because the Duke's undercover machinations have not endeared
him to her? If she accepts him, are we to believe she is in love with
him? There has been no hint of it. Is her independent spirit broken
so that she acquiesces with his plan just as she went along with the
bed-trick? Has this awkward, self-assured character been
assimilated into a romantic conclusion, or does she remain resolved
to follow her own path?

ANGELO

Much of Angelo's behaviour invites our hostility. His attempt to
take advantage of Isabella's desperate concern for her brother's life,
his lack of humanity in applying the law so harshly to Claudio, his
abandonment of a fiancée when her dowry is lost – these actions are
not designed to make him sympathetic. His personality in the play
is structured between the extremes of chastity and desire, as the man
whose 'urine is congealed ice' (Lucio, III.2.104) turns into 'an
hypocrite, a virgin-violator' (Isabella, V.1.41). It would be easy to
categorise Angelo as the moral crusader whose severity is directed at
others as a smokescreen for his own desires – the early modern
equivalent of the errant television evangelist or right-wing politician
whose public pronouncements on sexual morality are at odds with a
sleazy private life – but this is not the whole story. Certainly the
impression of the public Angelo is of a man holding himself in
check, whose speech is clipped and precise, and for whom self-
restraint is a way of life. Even the smile which seems to have been
characteristic (II.2.187, V.1.163, V.1.231) suggests a fixed, mask-like
expression, keeping the emotions and reactions under control.
Descriptions of him repeatedly use images which express

steadfastness, even rigidity: 'a man of stricture and firm abstinence' (I.3.12) who 'scarce confesses / That his blood flows' (I.3.52), 'whose blood / Is very snow-broth' (I.4.57), 'most strait in virtue' (II.1.9), 'severe' (II.1.269). Lucio talks of him needing to be 'soften[ed]' (I.4.70), and when Claudio describes the new governor as a rider showing his control over the horse of state with his spur (I.2.1158ff), the image could also serve for Angelo's relationship to his own animal desires. This language of restraint, of passions curbed, conforms to Angelo's own appearances in the play, and it is significant that he uses the corresponding imagery of release about his sexual desires: 'now I give my sensual race the rein' (II.4.160). His repressed emotions are violently released, hot and urgent from the pressure of constraint (see **Themes**, on **Freedom and restraint**).

Angelo is a man proud of his 'unsoiled name' (II.4.154): 'yea, my gravity, / Wherein let no man hear me, I take pride' (II.4.9–10), and while this pride may be a kind of **hubris**, the play does not suggest that he is serially hypocritical. He is a man once tempted, not habitually deceitful. (Were there any hint of previous slips in Viennese gossip, we might be sure that Lucio would broadcast it.) Yet the play sometimes seems to want to make him a symbol of the gap between appearance and reality: the word 'seem' and its variants are used about him (I.3.54, II.4.150, III.1.224), and the Duke emphasises his symbolic function through a pun on Angelo's name: 'O, what may man within him hide. / Though angel on the outward side' (III.2.259–60). The psychological subtlety of Angelo's characterisation, however, resists such a black-and-white reading. It is clear that Angelo is tormented rather than gratified by his desires. His lustful feelings towards Isabella seem to be a new and involuntary experience, and suddenly he understands the libidinous drives of his fellow men. His **soliloquy** after his first meeting with her shows in its broken rhythms and incessant questions the tatters of his iron self-possession. He recognises his temptation and struggles with it, railing against his own desires: 'what art thou, Angelo? / Dost thou desire her foully for those things / That make her good?' (II.2.173–5), and when his behaviour is revealed, he makes no excuses, craving 'death more willingly than mercy' (V.1.473). Programme notes from a production of the play by the Cheek by Jowl company in 1994 quoted from the twentieth-

> **CONTEXT**
>
> Some critics have seen in Angelo as representation of a puritan, or extreme protestant, rather like Shakespeare's characterisation of Malvolio in *Twelfth Night*.

century Italian poet and novelist, Cesare Pavese: 'We hate others because we hate ourselves'. Applied to Angelo, this might suggest that he punishes Claudio so harshly because he recognises, and despises, the same failings within himself. Angelo's characterisation is related to Claudio's through their parallel actions – the pre-contract between Angelo and Mariana echoes that between Claudio and Juliet, and at the end of the play Angelo's fate is seen to be dependent on Claudio's – 'An Angelo for Claudio' (V.1.406) – so that when Claudio is revealed to be alive, Angelo's life is saved (see **Themes**, on **Symmetry and antithesis**; **Substitution**). Angelo's preoccupation with self-restraint also links his presentation to that of Isabella.

If Angelo's faults are manifest, there are some redeeming features. At his first appearance he seems reluctant to take on the position of deputy, seeking for 'more test' (I.1.48). If the Duke does manufacture his promotion in order to verify his suspicions of Angelo's character, as 'what our seemers be' (I.3.54) may suggest, then Angelo's fall may seem to be forced on him. His interpretation of the law is indeed severe, but then that is what is demanded of him in a situation which has deteriorated under the laxity of the Duke's regime. He tries to operate according to the letter of the law, attempting to distance his private, individual self from his public, executive position: 'It is the law, not I, condemns your brother; / Were he my kinsman, brother, or my son, / It should be thus with him' (II.2.80–2). In his soliloquies he is painfully aware of his shortcomings, although seemingly powerless to control himself. He seems to experience partial repentance for the acts he believes are on his conscience, and his preoccupation with Claudio's supposed fate is clear in his speech at the end of IV.4, in which he twice expresses 'He should have lived' (IV.4.26, 30) without naming Claudio. This speech also shows his awareness of his acts, as well as an ambivalence towards them: 'Alack, when once our grace we have forgot, / Nothing goes right. We would, and we would not' (IV.4.31–2). In the final scene he is reduced to abject humiliation and shame, and prospects for his enforced marriage to Mariana do not seem bright. 'Love her, Angelo' (V.1.523), instructs the Duke, but there is no evidence in Angelo's cold, precise, disturbed characterisation that he is capable of it.

? QUESTION

'He was not an evil man; merely a weak one who fell into temptation.' Examine this view of Angelo.

CLAUDIO

Claudio speaks no lines at all at the end of the play. Yet at its heart, in III.1, he has a scene of extreme emotional and poetic intensity, in which some of the play's most fundamental philosophy is articulated. In a sense, Claudio is a minor character – a plot function whose presence is needed to motivate the actions and reveal the personalities of the play's major protagonists. He can be seen as a structural counterpoint to Mariana (see **Themes**, on **Symmetry and antithesis**), another plot- rather than personality-based intervention in the play. In his one big scene, however, Claudio resists the marginalisation which has made Mariana so two-dimensional.

Other characters view Claudio with approval and affection. Mistress Overdone says to Lucio and his companions that he 'was worth five thousand of you all' (I.2.60–1), Escalus calls him a 'gentleman' with 'a most noble father' (II.1.6–7), the Provost fervently wishes for his pardon (IV.2.68–9), Lucio declares he loved him (IV.3.155). His inherent decency is a necessary complication of the justice and punishment plot Shakespeare inherited from his sources (see **Sources**). The desire for restraint noted in the characters of Angelo and Isabella crops up again, more unexpectedly, in Claudio, who blames his crime on 'too much liberty' (I.2.124), for 'Our natures do pursue, / Like rats that ravin down their proper bane, / A thirsty evil, and when we drink we die' (I.2.127–9) (see **Themes**, on **Freedom and restraint**). Claudio both accepts his failings and the justice of his arrest, and repudiates the law for his punishment, just as in prison he oscillates wildly between stoic resignation and desperate panic. He seems caught between 'stiff upper lip' and human indignation and terror. In his interview with his sister, Claudio's repeated questions demonstrate his anxious search for a remedy to his situation. While expressing his readiness for death: 'I will encounter darkness as a bride. / And hug it in mine arms' (III.1.88), his mind is still turning over the possibilities for escape: 'Sure it is no sin' (III.1.113). His speech on death has an intensity which might be expected from a tragedy, and many critics have compared it to passages in *Hamlet*, and on his heartfelt plea 'Sweet sister, let me live' audiences may find their attitude towards Isabella's stance hardening. Claudio's characterisation is economical

CONTEXT

It has been argued that the stage direction which indicates Claudio enters Act 5 'muffled' refers to his wearing a shroud – marking him as somewhere between life and death.

but powerful, and his main functions are to question our judgements of other characters, especially Isabella and Angelo, and to humanise the play's discussion of abstract ideas of justice and mercy.

LUCIO

The cast-list published in the Folio describes Lucio as a 'fantastique' – one whose clothes or manners express eccentricity. Lucio's characteristic mode is rootlessness. He appears in six scenes and is a cynical, amoral character equally at home among the stews or in Angelo's apartments or in the prison. Some of the play's wittiest one-liners are given to him, as is its most severe punishment. Pompey calls him 'a gentleman' (III.2.39) and Lucio himself claims to have been an intimate of the Duke, but in fact he does not seem to fit into any single sphere or rank. His character is almost parasitic in its reliance on others: 'I am a kind of burr, I shall stick' (IV.3.175).

One of his principal functions is that of go-between. He is always going somewhere: to find out whether reports of Claudio's imprisonment are true, to seek Isabella, to Angelo. He wanders in and out of scenes, often alone. He claims 'Isabel, I loved thy brother' (IV.3.155), but will not stand bail for Pompey. Only his past liaison with Kate Keepdown suggests any kind of human contact, and his attitude towards her is crudely dismissive. In his first appearance, in I.2., he is joking about venereal disease – and this clever, cruel, edgy witticism is characteristic. When faced with Claudio's solemnity in the face of his arrest, Lucio's flippancy seems expressive of unease. He prefers 'the foppery of freedom' to 'the mortality of imprisonment' (I.2.132–3), and this disposition remains his watchword. He seems to have wriggled out of punishment and enjoys the freedom to mingle with different groups of people while his associates Claudio, Pompey and Mistress Overdone are all incarcerated. His next appearance is at the convent (I.4). In this encounter he seems to defer to Isabella's status, distinguishing his manners with her from his usual jesting dalliance with women (I.4.31–7). This is also marked by his use of the refined formality of verse speech unlike his habitual mocking prose. His account of 'your brother and his lover' (line 40) uses the imagery of natural fertility in contrast to the language of disease and commerce applied

CHECK THE FILM
In the BBC film of 1978, Lucio stands out from the other characters because of his costume: an elaborate and highly fashionable blue outfit which looks distinctly dandified amid the dreary colours of the prison and street settings.

to sex elsewhere in the play. In this scene he appears an astute judge of politics and character in his descriptions of the Duke and Angelo.

In his presence at the first meeting of Isabella and Angelo in II.2 his role is to urge her on, and in the initial exchange Lucio seems to feel much more desperation and tenacity about the project than she does. His repeated 'You are too cold' (II.2.45, 56) expresses his urgency. Neither Isabella nor Angelo gives any indication of having heard him, so that his promptings seem almost disembodied. In fact it is unclear whether he is speaking audibly to Isabella or whether his observations merely form a kind of commentary on the action – certainly Lucio is a character who often seems to be speaking with an ironic awareness of the audience. As Isabella's passion and eloquence grow, his comments are admiring and supportive. His comments on the Duke are humorous and much can be made of the **dramatic irony** of his slanders in performance. His unwitting remarks to the 'friar' may also generate audience sympathy for him.

He seems to enjoy the power that information and gossip can give him, even if it is made up. Even to Isabella, though, his assessment of the absent Duke is equivocal 'the old fantastical Duke of dark corners' (IV.3.155–6). In the final scene he adds some welcome levity with his constant comments – again, his is a kind of irreverent **choric** function and again he enjoys having and intervening with information, some of it false. His relation to the Duke is quite curious: his use of the word 'fantastical', recollecting the description of Lucio himself, seems to suggest a kind of equivalence between them. Both Lucio and the Duke are unattached characters and both enjoy the freedom to move between settings by which more orthodox characters would be constrained. Like the disguised Duke, Lucio is 'a looker-on here in Vienna' (V.1.315). When Lucio is accusing the disguised Duke of slandering the Duke, his scandalised interlocutor retorts 'you must, sir, change places with me, ere you make that my report' (V.1.333–4) (see **Themes**, on **Substitution**). Given this characteristic slipperiness, this shiftiness, it is not surprising that Lucio considers 'marrying a punk' as 'pressing to death, whipping and hanging' (V.1.519–20) – his forcible incorporation into the social institution of marriage expresses itself as the restraint of his very being.

 QUESTION

Lucio is hardly a virtuous figure, and yet he is consistently found likeable by readers and, more especially, audiences. How do you account for this?

THEMES

SYMMETRY AND ANTITHESIS

The title of the play, *Measure for Measure*, immediately introduces central idea of balance and equivalence. A common image for the process of law shows the scales of justice achieving a perfect balance, between mercy and punishment, between the severity of the crime and the severity of legal and social response. It has been suggested that Escalus's name alludes to this image, and the play also refers to it through weighing at III.2.254 and V.1.111 and in Angelo's taunt to Isabella: 'my false o'erweighs your true' (II.4.169–70). In some ways, *Measure for Measure* may be seen to seek an ideal balance, as it tries to reconcile the absolutes – the letter of the law for Angelo, chastity for Isabella, life or death for Claudio – which have motivated its characters and action. As the Duke remarks in the final scene, the law cries out for reparation: '"An Angelo for Claudio, death for death!" / Haste still pays haste, and leisure answers leisure, / Like doth quit like, and Measure still for Measure' (V.1.406–8). His words, in their use of the play's title, seem to resound as a kind of summary for the ethics of the whole piece. But if we look more closely at the context in which these lines are spoken, the idea of a just symmetry of crime and punishment is revealed to be more complicated than the formula of 'Measure for Measure' allows. The Duke invokes a false equivalence: Angelo's life might be placed in the balance against Claudio's, except that, as the audience knows, Claudio is not dead at all. By structuring this philosophy of justice on a conditional (see Substitution) – *if* Claudio *were* dead, Angelo's life *would be* payable in response – the play undermines its pronouncement. Given that Claudio is not dead, we don't quite know how a just punishment for Angelo might look, nor for what, under law, he is to be punished.

Other instances of apparent symmetry in the play also turn out to be unbalanced or disordered. Like Claudio, Lucio has got a woman pregnant outside marriage, but Lucio proudly parades his escape from his responsibilities. Angelo's precontractual relationship with Mariana mirrors Claudio's with Juliet, but Claudio wanted to marry Juliet whereas Angelo abandons his intended bride. In having what

> **CONTEXT**
>
> The Duke's words echo the biblical injunction 'an eye for an eye, a tooth for a tooth' (Matthew 5:38).

he believes is sex outside marriage, Angelo again revisits the actions of Claudio, but whereas the latter's crime 'was mutually committed' (II.3.27), Angelo's actions are surrounded by coercion and deceit. Repetitions in the plot, by which one situation or behaviour comments, through their similarity, on another, create much of the moral ambiguity of the play. Symmetries sometimes reveal themselves as antitheses: between liberty and restraint, between justice and mercy, between chastity and fornication, between eternal and earthly life. Although these opposites are bracketed together, they represent such extremes that no compromise or balance seems possible: *Measure for Measure* tends to dramatise incompatible belief systems rather than the possibility of a middle ground.

SUBSTITUTION

The theme of substitution is closely related to that of symmetry and antithesis: often alternatives which appear to be balanced actually require the substitution of one act or person for another. The whole plot is based on substitution – the replacement of the Duke by Angelo, and there are further substitutions, most notably the substitution of Mariana for Isabella in Angelo's bed, and the substitution of the head of Ragozine for that of Claudio in the prison. This last example involves two substitutions: first the head of Barnadine is proposed, and one effect of this added complication is to focus attention on this repeated theme. Both the bed-trick and the stay of execution of Claudio work through suggesting the interchangeability of persons. One can stand for another in a given situation: one dead head is very like another, and, more disturbingly, the play needs us to accept that bedding one woman is very like bedding another (as in the proverbial expression 'all cats are grey in the dark').

There are other kinds of substitution, too. Angelo's proposition to Isabella involves the substitution of her virginity for her brother's life. The pardon for Claudio which the Duke is expecting is substituted by a confirmation of his execution, and this in turn is substituted by the superior orders of the Duke. On a linguistic level, Elbow's **malapropisms** mistakenly substitute one word for another, and the inappropriateness of these verbal substitutions suggests that other substitutions are also unsatisfactory. Whipping is substituted

**CHECK
THE BOOK**
Terry Eagleton's book *William Shakespeare* (1986) discusses *Measure for Measure* in terms of exchange values and the difficulties of the tit-for-tat structures of justice and law.

QUESTION

Are all the substitutions in the play fair and justifiable?

for execution in the case of Lucio, and married life substituted for death for him and for Angelo. Perhaps Isabella substitutes the chaste and enclosed life of the convent for marriage to the Duke. The Duke himself substitutes a monk's habit for the robes of office. His final pronouncements substitute sex contained within marriage for extramarital relationships, in an attempt to substitute the nuclear family for the brothel and suburb.

When Isabella tries to persuade Angelo to be lenient, she begs him to put himself in her brother's situation, and thus to enact an imaginative self-substitution: 'If he had been as you, and you as he, / You would have slipped like him; but he, like you, / Would not have been so stern' (II.2.64–6). The emphasis on the shifting pronouns enacts, at the level of her **syntax**, the act of identification she seeks to prompt. Her plea for imaginative substitution, imagining oneself in the position of another, is also what is required of the play's audience. In order to become involved with the play's ethical questioning we need to imagine what we might do or how we might feel in the situation of the characters. This empathy shifts with the unfolding plot: one set of sympathies is substituted for another, as our responses to the characters develop. Escalus also asks Angelo to empathise with Claudio, wondering 'whether you had not sometime in your life / Erred in this point which now you censure him' (II.1.14–6). The irony in both cases is, of course, that Angelo will actually, not imaginatively, take the place of Claudio as fornicator and as prisoner awaiting execution. Isabella introduces her plea with the word 'If', a word which has a particular resonance in *Measure for Measure*. It pushes the play's philosophy into the territory of the conditional, the 'what if', and also towards a sense of bargaining, the 'if you … then I'. Both are appropriate for a play which produces ethical dilemmas and scenarios within a structure of substitution and antithesis.

FREEDOM AND RESTRAINT

One of the play's most fundamental thematic oppositions is between freedom and restraint, and as with many apparent oppositions, the distinctions between the two poles become increasingly blurred. On one level, freedom and restraint are physical states, represented by the brothel and the prison. Other physically restricted places are important to the play: Isabella wishes 'a more strict restraint' (I.4.4) in the enclosed convent of St Clare, although she never returns to it, and Mariana's 'moated grange' (III.1.265) and Angelo's 'garden circummured with brick' (IV.1.27) are both locations defined by enclosure, as indeed is Vienna itself (the Duke is to return to the city gates).

More significantly, however, these defined geographical spaces seem symbolic of inner, psychological restraint. It is entirely appropriate to Angelo's self-controlled character that he should have a walled garden (see **Characterisation**), and Mariana's willing immolation within her moated home shows how she has kept herself from the world since Angelo's desertion, but also how she has waited for him: 'His unjust unkindness, that in all reason should have quenched her love, hath, like an impediment in the current, made it more violent and unruly' (III.1.241–4). These secluded and surrounded habitations may also symbolise a virginal integrity, the unbroken and unentered body of chastity. Angelo refers to this association when he muses, after Isabella's departure, 'Shall we desire to raze the sanctuary / And pitch our evils there?' (II.2.171–2). Self-control, for both Angelo and Isabella, is both a freedom and a restraint (see **Characterisation**).

Freedom may seem an entirely positive state, but the play associates too much freedom with the perceived laxity and debauchery of Viennese society. Paradoxically, Claudio blames 'too much liberty' (I.2.124) for his arrest, arguing that human nature is not fit to regulate its own freedom: 'Our natures do pursue / Like rats that ravin down their proper bane, / A thirsty evil, and when we drink we die' (I.2.127–9). Angelo's government is described in terms of the rider's assertion of his authority over the unruly horse (I.2.158ff), and the imagery is repeated by the Duke at I.3.19–20 (see **Extended commentaries**, on **Text** 1): Vienna is a state which needs some restraint in order to enjoy freedom. As Claudio observes, 'every scope by the immoderate use / Turns to restraint' (I.2.126–7). Elsewhere, scope or expansiveness comes to mean restraint: when Isabella tells Claudio of the unacceptable price of his freedom, she uses the same opposition in 'a restraint, / Though all the world's vastidity you had, / To a determined scope' (III.1.71–3).

> **CONTEXT**
>
> Given this emphasis on restraint and repression, many productions have drawn on more recent association of Vienna as the home of psychoanalyst Sigmund Freud to explore these aspects.

Both life and death are represented in terms of freedom and restraint during the play. For Isabella, a sinful life is 'Perpetual durance' (III.1.70), freeing life but fettering the soul eternally. Claudio, on the other hand, sees death as being frozen in 'thick ribbèd ice, / To be imprisoned in the viewless winds' (III.1.126–7), despite being advised by the 'friar' that death is a release from burdensome life (III.1.4ff). At the end of the play, all the principals are released from prison or sentence, but are they, can they, and should they be, free?

CRIME, PUNISHMENT AND JUSTICE

The question of crime, punishment and justice is a major preoccupation of *Measure for Measure*. The law has swung like a pendulum from one extreme to another, from laxity to severity, and there seems to be no middle way. The Duke's final arrangement of affairs in the last act of the play begs as many questions as it answers. Many critics have felt that Angelo ought, in fairness, to be punished (see **Critical history**), although perhaps his public humiliation, his shattered self-image and his enforced marriage to Mariana are punishment enough. This apparent leniency contrasts with the threatened severity of Lucio's treatment. 'Slandering a prince' (V.1.521) appears to be the worst offence demanding the harshest penalty. For Angelo and Lucio, marriage is proposed as punishment (for men) and reward or deserts (for women), and the romantic side of marriage is tainted by this association. The pardoning of Barnadine, in whose case there are no mitigating factors and whose crime of murder far outweighs any other committed in the play, also casts doubt on the justice of the Duke's decrees. These last-act amnesties seem to bear little relation to the facts of the crimes committed.

This difficulty, of the appropriate balance between crime and punishment, runs through the play. Everything points to the unwarranted severity of Claudio's treatment, and Juliet's appearance in the play makes it clear that his behaviour is part of a consensual and committed relationship, rather than the violent acts of his prototype in the sources (see **Sources**) or the casual fornication of the brothel's clients. The play dramatises the difficulty of a just enforcement of the law. Angelo admits 'what knows the laws / That thieves do pass on thieves?' (II.1.22–3); Isabella maintains that only God 'is the top of judgement' (II.2.75), deferring earthly punishment. Angelo debates with Isabella and with Escalus the place of mercy or leniency in the law, sticking firmly to his view that it must not be made a 'scarecrow' on which birds perch unafraid (II.1.1), and while this is not in itself indefensible, the particular instances of its operation in the play do not foster our sympathy.

The play has a preponderance of courtroom scenes, and all these demonstrations of the legal process at work are unsatisfactory. In II.1, constable Elbow's repeated **malapropisms** and Pompey's timewasting speeches bring the proceedings down to a farce of unwitting puns and wordy filibustering. The matter of Elbow's wife, her pregnancy and her suspected (or is it respected? II.1.153ff) virtue entirely draw the attention away from the charges of bawding and pimping levelled at Pompey. Angelo's exasperated departure is preceded by a rare moment of wry humour – 'This will last out a night in Russia / When nights are longest there' (II.1.128–9), and Escalus is left to dispense justice. His verdict is feeble, if a pragmatic one, and Pompey's cheerful recognition that the commercial rewards of prostitution and the perennial attraction of casual sexual activity will always overrule the law casts the whole system into doubt. Nothing in the play contradicts his prediction that the law will not 'hold in Vienna ten year' (II.1.229–30), and the fact that he is arrested again in III.2 demonstrates the ineffectiveness of legal sanctions. The silence of the figure of Justice in II.1 is highly symbolic – and his only speech is to condemn Angelo rather than the malefactors (II.1.269). Even the Duke's fierce denunciation of Pompey in III.2.17ff seems to roll off its slippery target, as he continues his unrepentant jesting under the tutelage of the hangman Abhorson.

None of the play's persistent offenders seems to repent or show any hint of reformation: Barnadine, Pompey, and to some extent Lucio, show the limits of the law's power to enforce social and sexual morality in the face of such concerted criminality. There seems no reason to think that Vienna's moral crisis is over with the Duke's

> **CONTEXT**
>
> Shakespeare uses courtroom scenes in several of his plays – they are used to demonstrate authority (for example, in *Richard II*) or to increase the tension as the audience awaits the judgements (for example, in *The Merchant of Venice*).

**CHECK
THE BOOK**

*The Literary
Language of
Shakespeare*, by
S. S. Hussey (1982)
discusses
Shakespeare's
language in the
contexts of history,
poetry and rhetoric.

return to power, and nor is there any clarity about how he intends in future to avoid both the laxity of his previous regime and the severity of Angelo's interpretation of the law. The play judges the idea of justice and the conduct of those who seek to dispense it, as well as those who are on the receiving end.

IMAGERY AND LANGUAGE

Measure for Measure is written in a variety of styles, from the earthy, bawdy prose of Pompey to the shortened rhyming lines of the Duke's moralising commentary. Shifts between prose and verse are important and may comment on the status of the speakers (as in the difference between Claudio's **blank verse** philosophy and Lucio's prose jesting in I.2), but there is no clear class-based distinction between prose and verse speakers. Many of the play's characters, including the Duke, Escalus, Isabella and Claudio, use different forms at different points. End-rhyming is often employed to suggest proverbial wisdom, and in the mouth of the disguised Duke, the device has a quality almost of incantation (it has been pointed out that the rhyming couplets at III.2.175–8 and 249–70 echo the rhythms of the witches' spells in *Macbeth*.)

In a play preoccupied by sex, it is not surprising that bawdy and innuendo are the dominant features of the language of *Measure for Measure*. For some characters and in some situations, this is conscious, as in Lucio's punning on venereal diseases in I.2, and the slick and slippery language reveals and symbolises his moral shiftiness. Such language has, however, tainted the whole play. When Isabella tells Angelo 'I am come to know your pleasure' (II.4.31), even her modesty has been subconsciously affected by the prevailing language of sexual promiscuity and availability. Elsewhere, terms are overweighted with sexual meanings: the term 'pregnant', for example, used **metaphorically** by the Duke at I.1.11 and Angelo at II.1.23, also contains its literal meaning, particularly when the figure of the expectant mother Juliet, 'very near her hour' (II.2.16) serves as a visual reminder of the consequences of sexual activity. In addition to the language of sex, there are some passages of extended philosophic richness in the play: Claudio on his fear of

death, for example (III.1.121–135), or Isabella on the only true
judgement (II.2.73–9).

In her book *Shakespeare's Imagery and What it Tells us* (Cambridge
University Press, 1935), Caroline Spurgeon identifies a high
incidence of **personification** in the play. Many examples of this
figure involve images of the legal process, including 'liberty plucks
justice by the nose' (I.3.39), 'The law hath not been dead, though it
hath slept' (II.2.90) and 'The very mercy of the law cries out / Most
audible, even from his proper tongue' (V.1.404–5).

QUESTION

'The respective
merits of justice
and mercy and
explored in the
play, but no
overall view
emerges at the
end.' Discuss.

TREATMENT OF TIME

As with many of Shakespeare's plays, the timescale of *Measure for
Measure* seems inconsistent. For example, did the moral rot in
Vienna set in nineteen years previously, as Claudio tells us (I.2.167)
or only fourteen, as in the Duke's account (I.3.21)? How much time
do the events of the play take? An immediate chronology can be
established from indicators such as Lucio's promise to tell Isabella
of Claudio's arrest 'within two hours' (I.2.192) and her response
that she will bring news to her brother 'soon at night' (I.4.88). Lucio
offers to 'send after the Duke' (I.2.173), suggesting that he has not
been long gone. Angelo tells Isabella to attend him the next day
(II.2.160), and at that second meeting he again gives her a day's
grace: 'Answer me tomorrow' (II.4.167). Isabella vows to go to her
brother straight after this interview, and at the end of the scene of
their meeting the 'friar' sends her back to Angelo, bidding that 'If
for this night he entreat you to his bed, give him promise of
satisfaction' (III.1.263–4). There are numerous references to the date
and time of Claudio's execution, and this appointment is apparently
brought forward by Angelo's written command. The 'friar'
promises the Provost that the Duke will return within 'these two
days' (IV.2.192) and then tells that he 'comes home tomorrow'
(IV.3.126). As the plot develops under the Duke's orchestration,
events escalate into an almost unreal time-frame: the five lines given
to the Duke while Isabella tells Mariana about his plot in IV.1.59–64
are far too short to allow for the information to be conveyed.
Repeated injunctions to 'hurry' or 'go speedily' give an indication

CONTEXT

The time-scale of
Shakespeare's
plays was often
quite relaxed. For
example, in *A
Midsummer
Night's Dream*, the
opening lines state
that there are four
days till the
wedding, but we
can distinguish
only three.

of the quickening pace. And yet against this feeling that the Duke's absence may have been of only a few days' duration is the evidence that he knows Mariana well in his friar's disguise: she announces his arrival with 'Here comes a man of comfort, whose advice / Hath often stilled my brawling discontent' (IV.1.8–9). Similarly, Mistress Overdone's remark that 'Kate Keepdown was with child by [Lucio] in the Duke's time' (III.2.190–1) also suggests that Angelo's vice-governorship has been rather longer.

PART FOUR

CRITICAL HISTORY

EARLY RECEPTION

The earliest critics of *Measure for Measure* were somewhat nonplussed by this strange and powerful play: some were even offended or embarrassed by its frank depiction of illicit and coercive sexuality. Writing in the mid eighteenth century, Samuel Johnson considered that 'there is perhaps not one of Shakespear's plays more darkened than this by the peculiarities of its Authour', and that 'the plot is rather intricate than artful'. He also felt unhappy about the final judgement on Angelo: 'Angelo's crimes were such, as must sufficiently justify punishment ... and I believe every reader feels some indignation when he finds him spared.' A century later, the poet Samuel Taylor Coleridge went further, calling *Measure for Measure* 'a hateful work' and 'the single exception to the delightfulness of Shakspeare's plays'. Agreeing with Johnson on the morally unsatisfactory ending, Coleridge elaborated that 'our feelings of justice are grossly wounded in Angelo's escape. Isabella herself contrives to be unamiable, and Claudio is detestable.'

 CHECK THE BOOK
Coleridge generally admired Shakespeare's skill, referring in his lecture 'Shakespeare as Poet' to Shakespeare's 'unrivalled excellence'.

NINETEENTH-CENTURY CRITICISM

William Hazlitt, in his study *Characters of Shakespeare's Plays* (1817) was more favourable to the play, describing it 'as full of genius as it is of wisdom'. Like Coleridge, however, Hazlitt also found the main protagonists dislikeable, judging that 'there is, in general a want of passion; the affections are at a stand; our sympathies are repulsed and defeated in all directions'. Hazlitt identifies 'a general system of cross-purposes between the feelings of the different characters and the sympathy of the reader or audience', as he finds the Duke 'more absorbed in his own plots and gravity than anxious for the welfare of the state' and Isabella's 'rigid chastity' unappealing. For Hazlitt, the play's predominant 'principle of repugnance' reaches its height in the defiantly amoral character of Barnadine. Another expression of dissatisfaction with the play's resolution is found in the poet A.C.

Swinburne's *A Study of Shakespeare* first published in 1879.
Swinburne describes the audience's feelings: 'we are left hungry and
thirsty after having been made to thirst and hunger for some
wholesome single grain at least of righteous and too long retarded
retribution: we are tricked out of our dole, defeated of our due, lured
and led on to look for some equitable and satisfying upshot, defrauded
and derided and sent empty away.' In his reading, the play 'is in its
very inmost essence a tragedy', but its 'elaborate machinery' of plot
and its ingenuity are morally unworthy of Shakespeare's genius.

A late nineteenth-century perspective from Walter Pater gives a
more positive assessment of the play. Pater considered the quality of
Measure for Measure to be variable, but that this inconsistency
might account for 'some of that depth and weightiness which makes
this play so impressive, as with the true seal of experience, like a
fragment of life itself, rough and disjointed indeed, but forced to
yield in places its profounder meaning'. The play is, above all,
'indicative ... of Shakespeare's reason, of his power of moral
interpretation', inspiring the questions 'What philosophy of life,
what sort of equity?' For Pater, the play demonstrates 'the tyranny
of nature and circumstance over human action', where 'the
bloodless, impassible temperament does but wait for its
opportunity, for the almost accidental coherence of time with place,
and place with wishing, to annul its long and patient discipline, and
become in a moment the very opposite of that which under
ordinary conditions it seemed to be, even to itself'. 'The action of
the play,' Pater concluded, 'like the action of life itself ... develops
in us the conception of ... poetical justice, and the yearning to
realise it': 'as the play is full of the peculiarities of Shakespeare's
poetry, so in its ethics it is an epitome of Shakespeare's moral
judgements.' The *Casebook* on the play, edited by C.K. Stead
(Macmillan, 1971) contains useful extracts from early critics,
including Samuel Johnson and S.T. Coleridge.

**CHECK
THE BOOK**

Michael Mangan's
*A Preface to
Shakespeare's
Comedies* (1996)
covers
contemporary
definitions of
comedy in a lively
and accessible way.

STAGE HISTORY

If critics' response to the play as written literature was, at best,
guarded up to the end of the nineteenth century, so too were

attitudes to *Measure for Measure* as a piece for the stage. In the
Restoration period, the play was twice adapted, once by William
Davenant as *The Law Against Lovers* (1662), which interpolated the
Beatrice and Benedick plot from *Much Ado About Nothing*, and
again by Charles Gildon as *Measure for Measure, or Beauty the Best
Advocate* (1700). These adaptations were short lived, however, and
during the eighteenth century there were fairly regular productions
of Shakespeare's text, with major actors such as John Kemble as the
Duke and Mrs Cibber, Mrs Yates and Mrs Siddons as Isabella. Cuts
for performance meant the play was increasingly **bowdlerised**, with
Juliet's pregnancy only hinted at and the bed-trick so delicately
alluded to that it could easily be missed. During the nineteenth
century, the play's place in the repertory, never very firm, was
further eroded. It was not until the mid twentieth century that
Measure for Measure's dramatic potential was fully realised on the
stage. Peter Brook's production in 1950 was a landmark, in which
the contrasts between the 'religious thought' of the play's ideals and
the 'disgusting, stinking world of medieval Vienna' were
highlighted. The play's appeal to twentieth-century experience is
shown in the number of productions which have updated its setting,
often to the late nineteenth- or early twentieth-century Vienna of
the pioneer of psychoanalysis, Sigmund Freud.

Measure for Measure's stage history is surveyed in Graham
Nicholls's *Measure for Measure: Text and Performance* (Macmillan,
1986). Peter Brook's account of his 1950 production can be found in
his *The Empty Space* (1977); Juliet Stevenson and Paola Dionisotti
talk about their experiences of playing Isabella in *Clamorous Voices:
Shakespeare's Women Today* edited by Carol Rutter (The Women's
Press, 1988); and in Roger Smallwood and Russell Jackson's
volumes *Players of Shakespeare* (Cambridge University Press),
Roger Allam (in volume 3, 1993) and Daniel Massey (in volume 2,
1988) discuss the role of the Duke. Peter Corbin's essay 'Performing
Measure for Measure' in Nigel Wood, ed., *Measure for Measure*
(Open University, 1996) stresses that the play was written for
performance and that stage or film productions should be the 'initial
critical laboratory, not the study'. Adaptations of the play include
The Law for Lovers by William Davenant (1662), and, more
recently by Howard Brenton, whose version is published in *Three*

WWW. **CHECK
THE NET**
Find out more
about how
Shakespeare's plays
were printed and
their contexts at
**www.library.
upenn.edu/etext/
collections/
furness/eric/html**.

Plays edited by John Bull (Methuen, 1989). Bertolt Brecht's version of the play, performed in the early 1930s, converted it into *Die Rundkopfe und die Spitzkopfe* (*Round Heads and Pointed Heads*), a **Marxist** allegory in which the Duke represents capitalism and Angelo Hitler.

TWENTIETH-CENTURY VIEWS

The themes of *Measure for Measure* establish it as a play with particular resonances for the modern period, illustrating the playwright George Bernard Shaw's dictum, in his preface to *Plays Unpleasant* (1898), that in this play Shakespeare is 'ready and willing to start at the twentieth century if only the seventeenth would let him'. It is easy to see why its questioning stance has appealed to the sceptical twentieth century, in which the decline of religion and changing attitudes towards gender and sexuality have heightened its philosophical and dramatic potency. A modern willingness to enjoy its ambiguities and questions has also placed *Measure for Measure* at the centre of the critical and dramatic canon.

 CHECK THE BOOK
For a readable account of Shakespeare's life, work, and reputation, try Jonathan Bate's *The Genius of Shakespeare* (1997).

C.K. Stead's *Casebook* on the play includes some more recent essays by G. Wilson Knight on '*Measure for Measure* and the Gospels' (in which he argues for a Christian interpretation of the play with the Duke representing a divine principle of justice and mercy) and L.C. Knights on 'The Ambiguity of *Measure for Measure*' (which claims the play's incomplete clarification as a mark of its ethical and philosophical integrity). More recent criticism has tended to highlight Knights' interpretation, stressing questions rather than trying to supply answers: introductory studies by Harriet Hawkins (The Harvester Press, 1987) and Cedric Watts (Penguin, 1986) promote the play's contradictory ethics and moral relativism.

Recent essays written from distinct critical perspectives illuminate *Measure for Measure*. Jonathan Dollimore's 'Transgression and Surveillance in *Measure for Measure*' (in *Political Shakespeare: New Essays in Cultural Materialism* eds. Dollimore and Alan Sinfield, Manchester University Press, 1985) stresses a political reading of the play. It dramatises 'an exercise in authoritarian repression', in which the Duke's undercover surveillance of his people and a prevalent Christian morality that stigmatises sex as guilt combine to keep the populace under a sinister form of ideological control. Richard Wilson's 'Prince of Darkness: Foucault's Shakespeare' in Nigel Wood, ed., *Measure for Measure* (Open University, 1996), also stresses authoritarian control in his reading. He adapts the work of the French philosopher-historian, Michel Foucault, and in particular his writings on the rise of the prison as an instrument of social control, to present the Duke's surveillance as a version of the nineteenth-century invention of the Panopticon, a vantage point from which a large area could be surveyed and thereby controlled. It seems that few modern critics have a good word to say for the Duke.

In her book on Shakespeare written from a **feminist** perspective, 'Still Harping on Daughters: Women and Drama in the Age of Shakespeare' (Harvester Wheatsheaf, 1983), Lisa Jardine discusses the characterisation of Isabella in the context of Shakespeare's other female roles. She argues that his female characterisation is largely drawn from a range of stereotypes of feminine behaviour, and that while Isabella may seem to resist such stereotypes, her punishment is to be disliked by the play and its audiences. Nicholas Radel also considers the play 'Reading as a Feminist' in Nigel Wood's collection *Measure for Measure*, discussing how Isabella's sexuality is represented and how questions of gender form the basis of the play's argument.

 CHECK THE NET

The web page **http://www. theory.org.uk/ ctr-fouc.htm** gathers a range of critical resources on different critical approaches, including work influenced by Michel Foucault. It is good for general critical questions and methodology which you might be able to bring to the play.

PART FIVE

BACKGROUND

WILLIAM SHAKESPEARE'S LIFE

There are no personal records of Shakespeare's life. Official documents and occasional references to him by contemporary dramatists enable us to draw the main outline of his public life, but his private life remains hidden. Although not at all unusual for a writer of his time, this lack of first-hand evidence has tempted many to read his plays as personal records and to look in them for clues to Shakespeare's character and convictions. The results are unconvincing, partly because Renaissance art was not subjective or designed primarily to express its creator's personality, and partly because the drama of any period is very difficult to read biographically. Except when plays are written by committed dramatists to promote social or political causes (as by Shaw or Brecht), it is all but impossible to decide who amongst the variety of fictional characters in a drama represents the dramatist, or which of the various and often conflicting points of view expressed is authorial.

What we do know can be quickly summarised. Shakespeare was born into a well-to-do family in the market town of Stratford-upon-Avon in Warwickshire, where he was baptised, in Holy Trinity Church, on 26 April 1564. His father, John Shakespeare, was a prosperous glover and leather merchant who became a person of some importance in the town: in 1565 he was elected an alderman of the town, and in 1568 he became high bailiff (or mayor) of Stratford. In 1557 he had married Mary Arden. Their third child (of eight) and eldest son, William, learned to read and write at the primary (or 'petty') school in Stratford and then, it seems probable, attended the local grammar school, where he would have studied Latin, history, logic and rhetoric. In November 1582 William, then aged eighteen, married Anne Hathaway, who was twenty-six years old. They had a daughter, Susanna, in May 1583, and twins, Hamnet and Judith, in 1585.

CHECK THE BOOK

There are a number of biographies of Shakespeare – many of them very speculative – but the most authoritative is still Samuel Schoenbaum's *Shakespeare: A Documentary Life* (1975).

Shakespeare next appears in the historical record in 1592 when he is mentioned as a London actor and playwright in a pamphlet by the dramatist Robert Greene. These 'lost years' 1585–92 have been the subject of much speculation, but how they were occupied remains as much a mystery as when Shakespeare left Stratford, and why. In his pamphlet, *Greene's Groatsworth of Wit*, Greene expresses to his fellow dramatists his outrage that the 'upstart crow' Shakespeare has the impudence to believe he 'is as well able to bombast out a blank verse as the best of you'. To have aroused this hostility from a rival, Shakespeare must, by 1592, have been long enough in London to have made a name for himself as a playwright. We may conjecture that he had left Stratford in 1586 or 1587.

During the next twenty years, Shakespeare continued to live in London, regularly visiting his wife and family in Stratford. He continued to act, but his chief fame was as a dramatist. From 1594 he wrote exclusively for the Lord Chamberlain's Men, which rapidly became the leading dramatic company and from 1603 enjoyed the patronage of James I as the King's Men. His plays were extremely popular and he became a shareholder in his theatre company. He was able to buy lands around Stratford and a large house in the town, to which he retired about 1611. He died there on 23 April 1616 and was buried in Holy Trinity Church on 25 April.

SHAKESPEARE'S DRAMATIC CAREER

Between the late 1580s and 1613 Shakespeare wrote thirty-seven plays, and contributed to some by other dramatists. This was by no means an exceptional number for a professional playwright of the times. The exact date of the composition of individual plays is a matter of debate – the date of first performance is known for only a few plays – but the broad outlines of Shakespeare's dramatic career have been established. He began in the late 1580s and early 1590s by rewriting earlier plays and working with plotlines inspired by the Classics. He concentrated on comedies (such as *The Comedy of Errors*, 1590–4, which derived from the Latin playwright Plautus) and plays dealing with English history (such as the three parts of *Henry VI*, 1589–92), though he also tried his hand at bloodthirsty revenge tragedy (*Titus Andronicus*, 1592–3, indebted to both Ovid and Seneca). During the 1590s Shakespeare developed his expertise

www. CHECK THE NET
You can read Shakespeare's will in his own handwriting – and in modern transcription – online at the Public Records Office: **http://www.pro. gov.uk/ virtualmuseum** and search for 'Shakespeare'.

**CHECK
THE FILM**

There are lots of anachronisms and inaccuracies in *Shakespeare in Love* (1998) – that's half the fun of it – but its depiction of the hand-to-mouth world of the commercial theatre has something of the energy and edginess from which Shakespeare drew his artistic power.

in these kinds of plays to write comic masterpieces such as *A Midsummer Night's Dream* (1594–5) and *As You Like It* (1599–1600) and history plays such as *Henry IV* (1596–8) and *Henry V* (1598–9).

As the new century begins a new note is detectable. Plays such as *Troilus and Cressida* (1601–2) and *Measure for Measure* (1603–4), poised between comedy and tragedy, evoke complex responses. Because of their generic uncertainty and ambivalent tone such works are sometimes referred to as 'problem plays', but it is tragedy which comes to dominate the extraordinary sequence of masterpieces: *Hamlet* (1600–1), *Othello* (1602–4), *King Lear* (1605–6), *Macbeth* (1605–6) and *Antony and Cleopatra* (1606).

In the last years of his dramatic career, Shakespeare wrote a group of plays of a quite different kind. These 'romances', as they are often called, are in many ways the most remarkable of all his plays. The group comprises *Pericles* (1608), *Cymbeline* (1609–11), *The Winter's Tale* (1610–11) and *The Tempest* (1610–11). These plays (particularly *Cymbeline*) reprise many of the situations and themes of the earlier dramas but in fantastical and exotic dramatic designs which, set in distant lands, covering large tracts of time and involving music, mime, dance and tableaux, have something of the qualities of masques and pageants. The situations which in the tragedies had led to disaster are here resolved: the great theme is restoration and reconciliation. Where in the tragedies Ophelia, Desdemona and Cordelia die, the daughters of these plays – Marina, Imogen, Perdita, Miranda – survive and are reunited with their parents and lovers.

THE TEXTS OF SHAKESPEARE'S PLAYS

Nineteen of Shakespeare's plays were printed during his lifetime in what are called 'quartos': books, each containing one play, and made up of sheets of paper each folded twice to make four leaves. Shakespeare, however, did not supervise their publication. This was not unusual. When a playwright sold a play to a dramatic company he sold his rights in it: copyright belonged to whoever had possession of an actual copy of the text, and consequently authors had no control over what happened to their work. Anyone who

CONTEXT

A quarto is a small format book, roughly equivalent to a modern paperback. Play texts in quarto form typically cost sixpence, as opposed to the cost of going to the theatre at a penny.

could get hold of the text of a play might publish it if they wished. Hence, what found its way into print might be the author's copy, but it might be an actor's copy or prompt copy, perhaps cut or altered for performance; sometimes actors (or even members of the audience) might publish what they could remember of the text. Printers, working without the benefit of the author's oversight, introduced their own errors, through misreading the manuscript for example, and by 'correcting' what seemed to them not to make sense.

In 1623 John Heminges and Henry Condell, two actors in Shakespeare's company, collected together texts of thirty-six of Shakespeare's plays (*Pericles* was omitted) and published them in a large folio (a book in which each sheet of paper is folded once in half, to give two leaves). This, the First Folio, was followed by later editions in 1632, 1663 and 1685. Despite its appearance of authority, however, the texts in the First Folio still present many difficulties, for there are printing errors and confused passages in the plays, and its texts often differ significantly from those of the earlier quartos, when these exist.

Shakespeare's texts have, then, been through a number of intermediaries. We do not have the playwright's authority for any of his plays, and hence we cannot know exactly what it was that he wrote. Bibliographers, textual critics and editors have spent a great deal of effort on endeavouring to get behind the errors, uncertainties and contradictions in the available texts to recover the plays as Shakespeare originally wrote them. What we read is the result of these efforts. Modern texts are what editors have constructed from the available evidence: they correspond to no sixteenth- or seventeenth-century editions, and to no early performance of a Shakespeare play. Furthermore, these composite texts differ from each other, for different editors read the early texts differently and come to different conclusions. A Shakespeare text is an unstable and a contrived thing.

Often, of course, its judgements embody, if not the personal prejudices of the editor, then the cultural preferences of the time in which he or she was working. Growing awareness of this has led

---

CONTEXT

Plays were not considered as serious literature in this period: when, in 1612, Sir Thomas Bodley was setting up his library in Oxford he instructed his staff not to buy any drama for the collection: 'haply [perhaps] some plays may be worthy the keeping, but hardly one in forty.'

---

www. CHECK THE NET

You can find out more about the earliest editions of Shakespeare at the University of Pennsylvania's ERIC site: **http://oldsite. library.upenn.edu/ etext/collections/ furness/eric/eric. html**.

recent scholars to distrust the whole editorial enterprise and to repudiate the attempt to construct a 'perfect' text. Stanley Wells and Gary Taylor, the editors of the Oxford edition of *The Complete Works* (1988), point out that almost certainly the texts of Shakespeare's plays were altered in performance, and from one performance to another, so that there may never have been a single version. They note, too, that Shakespeare probably revised and rewrote some plays. They do not claim to print a definitive text of any play, but prefer what seems to them the 'more theatrical' version, and when there is a great difference between available versions, as with *King Lear*, they print two texts.

SHAKESPEARE AND THE ENGLISH RENAISSANCE

Shakespeare arrived in London at the very time that the Elizabethan period was poised to become the 'golden age' of English literature. Although Elizabeth reigned as queen from 1558 to 1603, the term 'Elizabethan' is used very loosely in a literary sense to refer to the period 1580 to 1625, when the great works of the age were produced. (Sometimes the later part of this period is distinguished as 'Jacobean', from the Latin form of the name of the king who succeeded Elizabeth, James I of England and VI of Scotland, who reigned from 1603 to 1625.) The poet Edmund Spenser heralded this new age with his pastoral poem *The Shepheardes Calender* (1579), and in his essay *An Apologie for Poetrie* (written about 1580, although not published until 1595) his friend Sir Philip Sidney championed the imaginative power of the 'speaking picture of poesy', famously declaring that 'Nature never set forth the earth in so rich a tapestry as divers poets have done ... Her world is brazen, the poet's only deliver a golden'.

CHECK THE NET

You can consult texts by Spenser and Sidney, and other contemporaries of Shakespeare, at Renascence Editions **http://www. uoregon.edu/ ~rbear/ren.htm**.

Spenser and Sidney were part of that rejuvenating movement in European culture which since the nineteenth century has been known by the term 'Renaissance'. Meaning literally 'rebirth' it denotes a revival and redirection of artistic and intellectual endeavour which began in Italy in the fourteenth century with the poetry of Petrarch. It spread gradually northwards across Europe, and is first detectable in England in the early sixteenth century in the writings of the scholar and statesman Sir Thomas More and in the poetry of Sir Thomas Wyatt and Henry Howard, Earl of Surrey. Its keynote was a curiosity in thought which challenged old assumptions and traditions. To the innovative spirit of the Renaissance, the preceding ages appeared dully unoriginal and conformist.

That spirit was fuelled by the rediscovery of many Classical texts and the culture of Greece and Rome. This fostered a confidence in human reason and in human potential which, in every sphere, challenged old convictions. The discovery of America and its peoples (Columbus had sailed in 1492) demonstrated that the world was a larger and stranger place than had been thought. The cosmological speculation of Copernicus (later confirmed by Galileo) that the sun, not the earth was the centre of our planetary system challenged the centuries-old belief that the earth and human beings were at the centre of the cosmos. The pragmatic political philosophy of Machiavelli seemed to cut politics free from its traditional link with morality by permitting to statesmen any means that secured the desired end. And the religious movements we know collectively as the Reformation broke with the Church of Rome and set the individual conscience, not ecclesiastical authority, at the centre of the religious life. Nothing, it seemed, was beyond questioning, nothing impossible.

Shakespeare's drama is innovative and challenging in exactly the way of the Renaissance. It examines and questions the beliefs, assumptions and politics upon which Elizabethan society was founded. And although the plays always conclude in a restoration of order and stability, many critics are inclined to argue that their imaginative energy goes into subverting, rather than reinforcing, traditional values. Frequently, figures of authority are undercut by some comic or parodic figure: against the Duke in *Measure for Measure* is set Lucio; against Prospero in *The Tempest*, Caliban; against Henry IV, Falstaff. Despairing, critical, dissident, disillusioned, unbalanced, rebellious, mocking voices are repeatedly to be heard in the plays, rejecting, resenting, defying the established order. They belong always to marginal, socially unacceptable figures, 'licensed', as it were, by their situations to say what would be unacceptable from socially privileged or responsible citizens. The

WWW. CHECK THE NET

The Luminarium site has links to a wide range of historical information on sixteenth-century topics including astronomy, medicine, economics and technology: **http:// www.luminarium. org.**

question is: are such characters given these views to discredit them, or were they the only ones through whom a voice could be given to radical and dissident ideas? Was Shakespeare a conservative or a revolutionary?

Renaissance culture was intensely nationalistic. With the break-up of the internationalism of the Middle Ages the evolving nation states which still mark the map of Europe began for the first time to acquire distinctive cultural identities. There was intense rivalry among them as they sought to achieve, in their own vernacular languages, a culture that could equal that of Greece and Rome. Spenser's great allegorical epic poem *The Faerie Queene*, which began to appear from 1590, celebrated Elizabeth and was intended to outdo the poetic achievements of France and Italy and to stand beside the works of Virgil and Homer. Shakespeare is equally preoccupied with national identity. His history plays tell an epic story that examines how modern England came into being through the conflicts of the fifteenth-century Wars of the Roses which brought the Tudors to the throne. He is fascinated, too, by the related subject of politics and the exercise of power. With the collapse of medieval feudalism and the authority of local barons, the royal court in the Renaissance came to assume a new status as the centre of power and patronage. It was here that the destiny of a country was shaped. Courts, and how to succeed in them, consequently fascinated the Renaissance; and they fascinated Shakespeare and his audience.

CHECK THE BOOK

Benedict Anderson's book on the rise of the nation and nationalism, *Imagined Communities* (revised ed., 1991), has been influential for its definition of the nation as 'an imagined political community' – imagined in part through cultural productions such as Shakespeare's history plays.

But the dramatic gaze is not merely admiring; through a variety of devices, a critical perspective is brought to bear. The court may be paralleled by a very different world, revealing uncomfortable similarities (for example, Henry's court and the Boar's Head tavern, ruled over by Falstaff in *Henry IV*). Its hypocrisy may be bitterly denounced (for example, in the diatribes of the mad Lear) and its self-seeking ambition represented disturbingly in the figure of a Machiavellian villain (such as Edmund in *Lear*) or a malcontent (such as Iago in *Othello*). Shakespeare is fond of displacing the court to another context, the better to examine its assumptions and pretensions and to offer alternatives to the courtly life (for example, in the pastoral setting of the forest of Arden in *As You Like It* or

Prospero's island in *The Tempest*). Courtiers are frequently figures of fun whose unmanly sophistication ('neat and trimly dressed, / Fresh as a bridegroom ... perfumed like a milliner', says Hotspur of such a man in *1 Henry IV*, I.3.33–6) is contrasted with plain-speaking integrity: Oswald is set against Kent in *King Lear*.

When thinking of these matters, we should remember that stage plays were subject to censorship, and any criticism had therefore to be muted or oblique: direct criticism of the monarch or contemporary English court would not be tolerated. This has something to do with why Shakespeare's plays are always set either in the past, or abroad.

The nationalism of the English Renaissance was reinforced by Protestantism. Henry VIII had broken with Rome in the 1530s and in Shakespeare's time there was an independent Protestant state church. Because the Pope in Rome had excommunicated Queen Elizabeth as a heretic and relieved the English of their allegiance to the crown, there was deep suspicion of Roman Catholics as potential traitors. This was enforced by the attempted invasion of the Spanish Armada in 1588. This was a religiously inspired crusade to overthrow Elizabeth and restore England to Roman Catholic allegiance. Roman Catholicism was hence easily identified with hostility to England. Its association with disloyalty and treachery was then reinforced by the Gunpowder Plot of 1605, a Roman Catholic attempt to destroy the government of England.

Shakespeare's plays are remarkably free from direct religious sentiment, but their emphases are Protestant. Young women, for example, are destined for marriage, not for nunneries (precisely what Isabella appears to escape at the end of *Measure for Measure*); friars are dubious characters, full of schemes and deceptions, if with benign intentions, as in *Much Ado About Nothing* or *Romeo and Juliet*. (We should add that Puritans, extreme Protestants, are even less kindly treated than Roman Catholics: for example, Malvolio in *Twelfth Night*).

The central figures of the plays are frequently individuals beset by temptation, by the lure of evil – Angelo in *Measure for Measure*,

CHECK THE FILM

We can get a modern equivalent of the effect of this displacement from Christine Edzard's film of *As You Like It* (1992). Here, the court scenes are set in the luxurious headquarters of a bank or company; the woodland scenes amid a sort of 'cardboard city' of social outcasts and the vulnerable.

Othello, Lear, Macbeth – and not only in tragedies: Falstaff is described as 'that old white-bearded Satan' (*1 Henry IV*, II.4.454). We follow their inner struggles. Shakespeare's heroes have the preoccupation with self and the introspective tendencies encouraged by Protestantism: his tragic heroes are haunted by their consciences, seeking their true selves, agonising over what course of action to take as they follow what can often be understood as a kind of spiritual progress towards heaven or hell.

SHAKESPEARE'S THEATRE

The theatre for which the plays were written was one of the most remarkable innovations of the Renaissance. There had been no theatres or acting companies during the medieval period. Performed on carts and in open spaces at Christian festivals, plays had been almost exclusively religious. Such professional actors as there were wandered the country putting on a variety of entertainments in the yards of inns, on makeshift stages in market squares, or anywhere else suitable. They did not perform full-length plays, but mimes, juggling and comedy acts. Such actors were regarded by officialdom and polite society as little better than vagabonds and layabouts.

Just before Shakespeare went to London all this began to change. A number of young men who had been to the universities of Oxford and Cambridge came to London in the 1580s and began to write plays that made use of what they had learned about the classical drama of ancient Greece and Rome. Plays such as John Lyly's *Alexander and Campaspe* (1584), Christopher Marlowe's *Tamburlaine the Great* (about 1587) and Thomas Kyd's *The Spanish Tragedy* (1588–9) were unlike anything that had been written in English before. They were full-length plays on secular subjects, taking their plots from history and legend, adopting many of the devices of Classical drama, and offering a range of characterisation and situation hitherto unattempted in English drama. With the exception of Lyly's prose dramas, they were composed in the unrhymed iambic pentameters (blank verse), which the Earl of Surrey had introduced into English earlier in the sixteenth century. This was a freer and more expressive medium than the rhymed verse

www. CHECK THE NET
Find out more about the Shakespearean theatre at **www.reading.ac. uk/globe**. This web site describes the historical researches undertaken in connection with the Globe theatre on London's Bankside, which was rebuilt in the late 1990s.

of medieval drama. It was the drama of these 'university wits' that Shakespeare challenged when he came to London. Greene was one of them, and we have heard how little he liked Shakespeare setting himself up as a dramatist.

The most significant change of all, however, was that these dramatists wrote for the professional theatre. In 1576 James Burbage built the first permanent theatre in England, in Shoreditch, just beyond London's northern boundary. It was called simply 'The Theatre'. Others soon followed. Thus, when Shakespeare came to London, there was a flourishing drama, theatres and companies of actors waiting for him, such as there had never been before in England. His company performed at James Burbage's Theatre until 1596, and used the Swan and Curtain until they moved into their own new theatre, the Globe, in 1599. It was burned down in 1613 when a cannon was fired during a performance of Shakespeare's *Henry VIII*.

With the completion in 1996 of Sam Wanamaker's project to construct in London a replica of the Globe, and with productions now running there, a version of Shakespeare's theatre can be experienced at first hand. It is very different to the usual modern experience of drama. The form of the Elizabethan theatre derived from the inn yards and animal baiting rings in which actors had been accustomed to perform in the past. They were circular wooden buildings with a paved courtyard in the middle open to the sky. A rectangular stage jutted out into the middle of this yard. Some of the audience stood in the yard (or 'pit') to watch the play. They were thus on three sides of the stage, close up to it and on a level with it. These 'groundlings' paid only a penny to get in, but for wealthier spectators there were seats in three covered tiers or galleries between the inner and outer walls of the building, extending round most of the auditorium and overlooking the pit and the stage. Such a theatre could hold about 3,000 spectators. The yards were about 80ft in diameter and the rectangular stage approximately 40ft by 30ft and 5ft 6in high. Shakespeare aptly called such a theatre a 'wooden O' in the prologue to *Henry V* (line 13).

The stage itself was partially covered by a roof or canopy, which projected from the wall at the rear of the stage and was supported

CHECK THE BOOK

The most authoritative book on what we know about the theatre of Shakespeare's time is Andrew Gurr's *The Shakespearean Stage* (1992).

CONTEXT

Whereas now we would conceptualise a visit to the theatre as going to *see* a play, the most common Elizabethan phrase was 'to go *hear* a play' (as in *The Taming of the Shrew*, Induction 2.130) – thus registering the different sensory priorities of the early modern theatre.

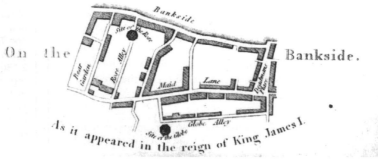

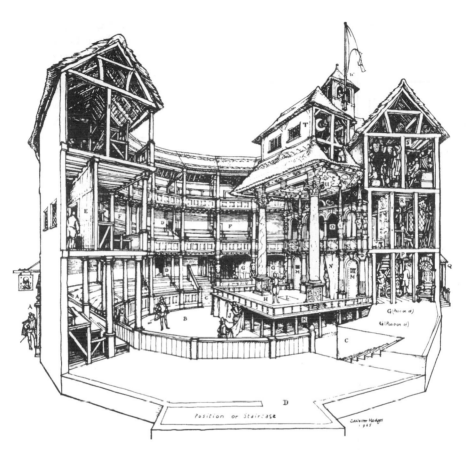

A CONJECTURAL RECONSTRUCTION OF THE INTERIOR OF THE GLOBE PLAYHOUSE

AA	Main entrance	N	Curtained 'place behind the stage'
B	The Yard	O	Gallery above the stage, used as required
CC	Entrances to lowest galleries		sometimes by musicians, sometimes by
D	Entrance to staircase and upper galleries		spectators, and often as part of the play
E	Corridor serving the different sections of the	P	Back-stage area (the tiring-house)
	middle gallery	Q	Tiring-house door
F	Middle gallery ('Twopenny Rooms')	R	Dressing-rooms
G	'Gentlemen's Rooms or Lords Rooms'	S	Wardrobe and storage
H	The stage	T	The hut housing the machine for lowering
J	The hanging being put up round the stage		enthroned gods, etc., to the stage
K	The 'Hell' under the stage	U	The 'Heavens'
L	The stage trap, leading down to the Hell	W	Hoisting the playhouse flag
MM	Stage doors		

CONTEXT

We do not know much about the props list for a theatre company in Shakespeare's time, although the evidence we do have suggests that there were some quite ambitious examples: one list dating from 1598 includes decorated cloths depicting cities or the night sky, items of armour, horses' heads and 'one hell mouth', probably for performances of Marlowe's famous play *Doctor Faustus*.

by two posts at the front. This protected the stage and performers from inclement weather, and to it were secured winches and other machinery for stage effects. On either side at the back of the stage was a door. These led into the dressing room (or 'tiring house') and it was by means of these doors that actors entered and left the stage. Between these doors was a small recess or alcove which was curtained off. Such a 'discovery place' served, for example, for Juliet's bedroom when in Act IV Scene 4 of *Romeo and Juliet* the Nurse went to the back of the stage and drew the curtain to find Juliet apparently dead on her bed. Above the discovery place was a balcony, used for the famous balcony scenes of *Romeo and Juliet* (II.2 and III.5), or for the battlements of Richard's castle when he is confronted by Bolingbroke in *Richard II* (III.3). Actors (all parts in the Elizabethan theatre were taken by boys or men) had access to the area beneath the stage; from here, in the 'cellarage', would have come the voice of the ghost of Hamlet's father (*Hamlet*, II.1.150–82).

On these stages there was very little in the way of scenery or props – there was nowhere to store them (there were no wings in this theatre) nor any way to set them up (no tabs across the stage), and, anyway, productions had to be transportable for performance at court or at noble houses. The stage was bare, which is why characters often tell us where they are: there was nothing on the stage to indicate location. It is also why location is so rarely topographical, and much more often symbolic. It suggests a dramatic mood or situation, rather than a place: Lear's barren heath reflects his destitute state, as the storm his emotional turmoil.

None of the plays printed in Shakespeare's lifetime marks act or scene divisions. These have been introduced by later editors, but they should not mislead us into supposing that there was any break in Elizabethan performances such as might happen today while the curtains are closed and the set is changed. The staging of Elizabethan plays was continuous, with the many short 'scenes' of which Shakespeare's plays are often constructed following one after another in quick succession. We have to think of a more fluid, and much faster, production than we are generally used to: in the prologues to *Romeo and Juliet* (line 12) and *Henry VIII* (line 13)

Shakespeare speaks of the playing time as only two hours. It is because plays were staged continuously that exits and entrances are written in as part of the script: characters speak as they enter or leave the stage because otherwise there would be a silence while, in full view, they took up their positions. (This is also why dead bodies have to be carried off: they cannot get up and walk off.)

In 1608 Shakespeare's company, the King's Men, acquired the Blackfriars Theatre, a smaller, rectangular indoor theatre, holding about 700 people, with seats for all the members of the audience, facilities for elaborate stage effects and, because it was enclosed, artificial lighting. It has been suggested that the plays written for this 'private' theatre differed from those written for the Globe, since, as it cost more to go to a private theatre, the audience came from a higher social stratum and demanded the more elaborate and courtly entertainment which Shakespeare's romances provide. However, the King's Men continued to play at the Globe in the summer, using Blackfriars in the winter, and it is not certain that Shakespeare's last plays were written specifically for the Blackfriars theatre, or first performed there.

READING SHAKESPEARE

Shakespeare's plays were written for this stage, but there is also a sense in which they were written *by* the stage. The material and physical circumstances of their production in such theatres had a profound effect upon the nature of Elizabethan plays. Unless we bear this in mind, we are likely to find them very strange, for we will read with expectations shaped by our own familiarity with modern fiction and modern drama which is, by and large, realistic; it seeks to persuade us that what we are reading or watching is really happening. This is quite foreign to Shakespeare. If we try to read him like this, we shall find ourselves irritated by the improbabilities of his plot, confused by his chronology, puzzled by locations, frustrated by unanswered questions and dissatisfied by the motivation of the action. The absurd ease with which disguised persons pass through Shakespeare's plays is a case in point: why does no one recognise people they know so well? There is a great deal of psychological accuracy in Shakespeare's plays, but we are far from any attempt at realism.

 CHECK THE BOOK
Deborah Cartmell's *Interpreting Shakespeare on Screen* (2000) is recommended for its clear and interesting sense of the possibilities and the requirements of approaching Shakespeare through the cinema.

CONTEXT

The Romantic critic S. T. Coleridge argued that literature requires our 'willing suspension of disbelief': but it is not clear that the theatre of the Shakespearean period did require its audience to forget that they were in a theatre. Certainly, remarks calling attention to the theatrical setting are commonplace – in comedies such as *Twelfth Night* (III.4.125) and *As You Like It* II.7.139–43, and in tragedies including *Macbeth* (V.5.23–5) – making it more difficult to forget the theatricality of the stories depicted.

The reason is that in Shakespeare's theatre it was impossible to pretend that the audience was not watching a contrived performance. In a modern theatre, the audience is encouraged to forget itself as it becomes absorbed by the action on stage. The worlds of the spectators and of the actors are sharply distinguished by the lighting: in the dark auditorium the audience is passive, silent, anonymous, receptive and attentive; on the lighted stage the actors are active, vocal, demonstrative and dramatic. (The distinction is, of course, still more marked in the cinema.) There is no communication between the two worlds: for the audience to speak would be interruptive; for the actors to address the audience would be to break the illusion of the play. In the Elizabethan theatre, this distinction did not exist, and for two reasons: first, performances took place in the open air and in daylight which illuminated everyone equally; secondly, the spectators were all around the stage (and wealthier spectators actually on it), and were dressed no differently from the actors, who wore contemporary dress. In such a theatre, spectators would be as aware of each other as of the actors; they could not lose their identity in a corporate group, nor could they ever forget that they were spectators at a performance. There was no chance that they could believe 'this is really happening'.

This, then, was communal theatre, not only in the sense that it was going on in the middle of a crowd but also in the sense that the crowd joined in. Elizabethan audiences had none of our deference: they did not keep quiet, nor arrive on time, nor remain for the whole performance. They joined in, interrupted, even getting on the stage. And plays were preceded and followed by jigs and clowning. It was all much more like our experience of a pantomime, and at a pantomime we are fully aware, and are meant to be aware, that we are watching games being played with reality. The conventions of pantomime revel in their own artificiality: the fishnet tights are to signal that the handsome prince is a woman, the Dame's monstrous false breasts signal that 'she' is a man.

Something very similar is the case with Elizabethan theatre: it utilised its very theatricality. Instead of trying to persuade spectators that they are not in a theatre watching a performance,

Elizabethan plays acknowledge the presence of the audience. It is addressed not only by prologues, epilogues and choruses, but also in soliloquies. There is no realistic reason why characters should suddenly explain themselves to empty rooms, but, of course, there is no empty room. The actor is surrounded by people. Soliloquies are not addressed to the world of the play; they are for the audience's benefit. And that audience's complicity is assumed: when a character like Prospero declares himself to be invisible, it is accepted that he is. Disguises are taken to be impenetrable, however improbable, and we are to accept impossibly contrived situations, such as barely hidden characters remaining undetected (indeed, on the Elizabethan stage there was nowhere at all they could hide).

These, then, are plays that are aware of themselves as dramas; in critical terminology, they are self-reflexive, commenting upon themselves as dramatic pieces and prompting the audience to think about the theatrical experience. They do this not only through their direct address to the audience but also through their fondness for the play-within-a-play (which reminds the audience that the encompassing play is also a play) and their constant use of images from, and allusions to, the theatre. They are fascinated by role-playing, by acting, appearance and reality. Things are rarely what they seem, either in comedy (for example, in *A Midsummer Night's Dream*) or tragedy (*Romeo and Juliet*). This offers one way to think about those disguises: they are thematic rather than realistic. Kent's disguise in *Lear* reveals his true, loyal self, while Edmund, who is not disguised, hides his true self. In *As You Like It*, Rosalind is more truly herself disguised as a man than when dressed as a woman.

www. CHECK
THE NET
The 'Designing Shakespeare' database at PADS (**www.pads.ahds. ac.uk**) has an extensive collection of photographs from different productions available online.

The effect of all this is to confuse the distinction we would make between 'real life' and 'acting'. The case of Rosalind, for example, raises searching questions about gender roles, about how far it is 'natural' to be womanly or manly: how does the stage, on which a man can play a woman playing a man (and have a man fall in love with him/her), differ from life, in which we assume the roles we think appropriate to masculine and feminine behaviour? The same is true of political roles: when a Richard II or Lear is so aware of the regal part he is performing, of the trappings and rituals of kingship, their plays raise the uncomfortable possibility that the answer to the

CONTEXT

The poet Walter Raleigh wrote a poem on this image of life as theatre, which begins 'What is our life? A play of passion', in which 'Our mothers' wombs the tiring houses be, / Where we are dressed for this short comedy'. There's a twist at the end of the short verse: 'Only we die in earnest, that's no jest.'

question of what constitutes a successful king is simply: a good actor. Indeed, human life generally is repeatedly rendered through the imagery of the stage, from Macbeth's 'Life's but a walking shadow, a poor player / That struts and frets his hour upon the stage / And then is heard no more' (V.5.23–5) to Prospero's paralleling of human life to a performance which, like the globe (both world and theatre!) will end (IV.I.146–58). When life is a fiction, like this play, or this play is a fiction like life, what is the difference? 'All the world's a stage...' (*As You Like It*, II.7.139).

SOURCES

A popular moral tale current in Shakespeare's day provides the plot of *Measure for Measure*. It exists in various forms which share a basic outline. A beautiful woman goes to an official to plead for a pardon for her husband, languishing in prison under sentence of death. The official offers the pardon if she will spend the night with him. The wife agrees, reluctantly, and after she has fulfilled her part of the bargain, the official orders the execution of her husband. She complains of this treatment to some higher authority, a lord or duke, who punishes the official by forcing him to marry her, endow her with his property, and then executes him for his treachery. Many versions of the story presented it as a Protestant morality in which the duke or lord represented a supreme wisdom, but others see his enactment of justice as unduly severe.

One version of the story known by Shakespeare was that by the Italian Giovanni Giraldi Cinthio, first published in 1565. (Shakespeare also used a plot from Cinthio's collection of stories *Hecatommithi* for *Othello*.) In Cinthio's telling of this tale, the woman is sister, not wife, to the condemned man, and her beauty and intelligence make her the central character in the narrative. Her brother is sixteen years old and in prison for rape – a crime punishable by death even though he expresses himself willing to marry his victim. The official, by contrast, has no intention of marrying the woman, seeing instead only the possibility of gratifying his own lusts. When the story emerges, he is condemned to marry her, and then she successfully pleads for his life.

This outline of Cinthio's narrative shows how Shakespeare departed from his source in certain key ways. One is his softening of the crime for which Claudio is imprisoned – the mutual act of extra-marital sex rather than the coercive violence of rape. Another is his elaboration of Isabella's chaste instincts by giving her a religious vocation, and his decision to allow her to retain her chastity through the device of the bed-trick. Cinthio's story was the source for a probably unperformed play by George Whetstone, *Promos and Cassandra* (1578), also used by Shakespeare in writing *Measure for Measure*. Whetstone adds a comic, lowlife subplot which may well have inspired Shakespeare, and he also allows the condemned brother to escape execution through the substitution of a head of another executed prisoner. In Whetstone's version it is not quite clear whether the brother's crime was consensual, as in *Measure for Measure*, or violent, as in *Hecatommithi*, but he, like Claudio, is sentenced under the provisions of an old law which has been allowed to lapse.

In collating and elaborating these versions of the existing story, Shakespeare seems to have had certain distinct purposes. First, he interrelates the different elements of the plot largely through introducing symmetries: parallels between the Duke and Angelo, Angelo and Claudio, Claudio and Isabella, Isabella and Mariana (see **Themes**, on **Symmetry and antithesis**). Secondly he extends the role of the Duke by making him the unseen observer of events, rather than, as in Whetstone's play, a *deus ex machina* figure who makes a ceremonial and authoritative entry to dispense justice at the end of the play. Thirdly he makes moral questions central to his drama. In *Measure for Measure*, more than in any of Shakespeare's sources, we are required to think about the issues raised and we also need to be prepared to shift our sympathies from one character to another.

Other elements of *Measure for Measure* may have their genesis in different kinds of texts. Shakespeare seems to have borrowed from himself for the bed-trick – the substitution (see **Themes**, on **Substitution**) of Mariana for Isabella in Angelo's bed – as this device also occurs in his *All's Well that Ends Well*. There are significant biblical sources too: the play's title echoes the Sermon on

> **CONTEXT**
>
> In Greek drama a Deus ex machina was a god lowered on to the stage by a piece of machinery, if such an intervention was needed to assist or complete the unfolding of the plot. The term is used to describe any unexpected or improbable intervention to resolve the action.

the Mount. In the account in Matthew's gospel, Jesus tells his followers 'Judge not, that ye be not judged. For with what judgement ye judge, ye shall be judged; and with what measure ye mete, it shall be measured to you again' (Matthew 7:1–2). Christ warns against judging others harshly without looking at one's own faults: 'Thou hypocrite, first cast out the beam out of thine own eye; and then thou shalt see clearly to cast out the mote out of thy brother's eye' (7:5). The version in Luke's gospel urges Christians: 'Be ye therefore merciful, as your Father also is merciful. Judge not, and ye shall not be judged: condemn not, and ye shall not be condemned: forgive, and ye shall be forgiven. Give, and it shall be given unto you; good measure, pressed down, and shaken together, and running over, shall men give into your bosom. For with the same measure that ye mete withal it shall be measured to you again' (Luke 6:36–8).

CHECK THE NET

You can look at an online version of the Geneva Bible at **http://www. genevabible.org/ Geneva.html**.

World events	Shakespeare's life (*dates for plays are approximate*)	Literature and the arts
1492 Columbus sets sails for America		
		1513 Niccolò Machiavelli, *The Prince* (source)
		1528 Castiglione's *Book of the Courtier*
		1532 Ariosto's *Orlando Furioso*
1534 Henry VIII breaks with Rome		
1556 Archbishop Cranmer burnt at the stake		
1558 Elizabeth I accedes to throne		
		1562 Lope de Vega, great Spanish dramatist, born
	1564 (26 April) **William Shakespeare** baptised, Stratford-upon-Avon	
		1565 Giambattisa Giraldi Cinzio, *The Hecatommithi* (source)
1570 Elizabeth I excommunicated by Pope Pius V		
	1576 James Burbage builds the first theatre in England, at Shoreditch	
1577 Francis Drake sets out on voyage round the world		
		1578 George Whetstone, *Promos and Cassandra* (source)
		1580 (c.) Sir Philip Sidney, *An Apologie for Poetrie*
	1582 Shakespeare marries Anne Hathaway	
	1583 His daughter, Susanna, is born	
1584 Ralegh's sailors land in Virginia		
	1585 His twins, Hamnet and Judith, are born	
1587 Execution of Mary Queen of Scots	**late 1580s–early 1590s** Probably writes *Henry VI* (Parts I, II, III) and *Richard III*	

continued

World events	Shakespeare's life (*dates for plays are approximate*)	Literature and the arts
		1588–9 Thomas Kyd, *The Spanish Tragedy*
1588 The Spanish Armada defeated		
		1590 Edmund Spenser, *The Faerie Queene* (Books I–III)
1592 Plague in London closes theatres	**1592** Recorded as being a London actor and an 'upstart crow'	
	1592–4 Writes *Comedy of Errors*	
	1594 onwards Writes exclusively for the Lord Chamberlain's Men.	
	1595 (pre) *Two Gentleman of Verona, The Taming of the Shrew* and *Love's Labour's Lost* probably written	
	1595 (c.) *Romeo and Juliet,*	
1596 English raid on Cadiz	**1596–8** First performance, *The Merchant of Venice*	
	1598–9 Globe Theatre built at Southwark	
	1599 *Henry V*	**1599** Thos Heywood (?), *Edward IV*
	1600 *A Midsummer Night's Dream, Much Ado About Nothing* and *The Merchant of Venice* printed in quartos	
	1600–1 *Hamlet*	
	1601 Writes *Troilus and Cressida*	**1601** Ben Jonson, *Cynthia's Revels*
	1600–2 *Twelfth Night*	
	1602–4 Probably writes *Othello*	
1603 Death of Queen Elizabeth Tudor; accession of James Stuart; law passed to demolish brothels in suburbs to prevent spread of Plague	**1603 onwards** His company enjoys patronage of James I as The King's Men	
	1604 '*Mesur for Mesur*' by 'Shaxberd' performed at Palace of Whitehall; *Othello* performed	

World events	Shakespeare's life (*dates for plays are approximate*)	Literature and the arts
1605 Discovery of Guy Fawkes' plot	**1605** First version of *King Lear*	**1605** Cervantes, *Don Quijote de la Mancha*
	1606 *Macbeth*	
	1606-7 *Antony and Cleopatra*	
	1608 The King's Men acquire Blackfriars Theatre for winter performances	
1609 Galileo constructs first astronomical telescope		**1609** Beaumont & Fletcher *The Philastor, or Love Lies-a-Bleeding*
1610 William Harvey discovers circulation of blood		
	1611 *Cymbeline, The Winter's Tale* and *The Tempest* performed	
1612 Last burning of heretics in England	**1612** Shakespeare retires from London theatre and returns to Stratford	**1612** John Webster, *The White Devil*
	1613 The Globe Theatre burns down	
	1616 Death of William Shakespeare	
1618 Thirty Years War begins in England		
		1622 Birth of French dramatist Molière
	1623 First Folio of Shakespeare's works includes *Measure for Measure* as a comedy	

EDITIONS OF *MEASURE FOR MEASURE*

N. W. Bawcutt, *Measure for Measure,* Clarendon Press, Oxford, 1991

Brian Gibbons (ed.), *Measure for Measure,* Cambridge University Press, Cambridge, 1991

COLLECTIONS OF ESSAYS AND ARTICLES

George L. Geckle (ed.), *Twentieth century interpretations of Measure for Measure: a collection of critical essays*, Prentice-Hall, Englewood Cliffs, N.J., 1970

C. K. Stead (ed.), *Shakespeare: Measure for Measure: a casebook*, Macmillan, London, 1971

T. F. Wharton, *Measure for Measure: The Critics Debate*, Macmillan, Basingstoke, 1989

Nigel Wood (ed.), *Measure for Measure,* Open University Press, Buckingham, 1995

CRITICAL STUDIES

Kate Chedgzoy, *Measure for Measure,* Northcote House in association with the British Council, Tavistock, 2000

Harriett Hawkins, *Measure for Measure*, Harvester, Brighton, 1987

Rosalind Miles, *The Problem of Measure for Measure: a historical investigation*, Vision Press London, 1976

Graham Nicholls, *Measure for Measure: text and performance,* Macmillan, Basingstoke, 1986

STUDIES CONSIDERING THE PLAY ALONGSIDE OTHER WORKS

Cicely Barry, *The Actor and His Text*, Virgin Books, London, 1987

Peter Brook, *The Empty Space*, Penguin, London, 1977

David Crystal, Ben Crystal, Stanley Wells, *Shakespeare's Words*, Penguin, London, 2003

Terry Eagleton, *William Shakespeare*, Blackwell, Oxford, 1986

S. S. Hussey, *The Literary Language of Shakespeare*, Longman, Harlow, 1982

Frank Kermode, *Shakespeare's Language*, Penguin, London, 2001

Michael Mangan, *A Preface to Shakespeare's Comedies: 1594-1603*, Longman, Harlow, 1996

Nicholas Marsh, *Shakespeare: three problem plays*, Palgrave Macmillan, Basingstoke, 2002

Russ McDonald, *Shakespeare and the Arts of Language*, Oxford University Press, Oxford, 2001

Patsy Rodenburg, *Speaking Shakespeare*, Methuen, London, 2002

Carol Rutter et al., *Clamorous Voices: Shakespeare's Women Today*, The Women's Press, London, 1987

Emma Smith (ed.), *Blackwell Guides to Criticism: Shakespeare's Comedies*, Blackwell, Oxford, 2003

John Sutherland, Cedric Watts, Stephen Orgel, *Henry V, War Criminal? And Other Shakespeare Puzzles*, Oxford World Classics, Oxford, 2000

STUDIES OF SHAKESPEARE'S LIFE

Jonathan Bate, *The Genius of Shakespeare*, Picador, London, 1997

Samuel Schoenbaum, *Shakespeare: A Documentary Life*, Oxford University Press, 1975

LITERARY TERMS

aside a non-naturalistic dramatic convention allowing characters to voice their thoughts, sometimes addressing the audience directly, without other characters hearing them

blank verse unrhymed **iambic pentameter**

bowdlerised expurgated, from Dr Thomas Bowdler's *Family Shakespeare* (1818) 'in which those words or expressions are omitted which cannot without propriety be read aloud in a family'

choric in ancient Greek tragedies a chorus was a group of characters who observed the action and commented on it but were not involved or active within it. Choric characters in other types of play tend to be observers rather than participants, and their ironic insights direct the audience's understanding of the events of the drama. Other Shakespearean characters sometimes ascribed a choric function are Enobarbus in *Antony and Cleopatra* and the Fool in *King Lear*

couplet pair of rhymed lines. End-rhyme is common in early Shakespeare plays such as *Richard II* and *The Comedy of Errors* but by the time of *Measure for Measure* it is less frequently employed and therefore worth examining to determine why this form has been chosen

dénouement the final unfolding of a plot

dramatic irony a commonly used device by which the audience possesses more information about events than the characters themselves. In comedy this knowledge is often a source of humour

feminist criticism a way of reading literature by stressing the role of gender in the text, its production and its reception

gnomic verse containing maxims of popular wisdom, short, impressive statements of general truths

hubris the complacent self-confidence that causes a tragic hero to ignore the laws and warnings of the gods and therefore defy them to bring about his or her downfall

hyperbole a figure of speech which gives emphasis through exaggeration

iambic pentameter an iamb is a metrical foot consisting of a weak stress followed by a strong stress, ti-tum. There are five of these in a line of iambic pentameter

Machiavellian adjective derived from Renaissance perceptions of the works of Florentine writer Niccolo Machiavelli (1469–1527), who wrote a book of political advice to rulers called *The Prince* (1513). In this work he recommended preserving power by manipulating the populace

malapropism mistaken and muddled use of long words: so called after Mrs Malaprop in Sheridan's play *The Rivals* (1775) who constantly utters nonsense in her attempts to sound learned. As well as in *Measure for Measure*, Shakespeare uses the device to characterise the comic constable Dogberry in *Much Ado About Nothing*

Marxist criticism criticism that considers literature in relation to its capacity to reflect the struggle between the classes, and the economic conditions which, according to Karl Marx (1818–83) and Friedrich Engels (1820–95), lie at the basis of man's intellectual and social evolution

metaphor a comparison between two things or ideas, made by fusing them together: one thing is described as being another thing, thus carrying over its associations: e.g. 'The needful bits and curbs to headstrong weeds' (I.3.20)

peripeteia in comedy, a sudden change in events for the better

personification a figure of speech in which things or abstract ideas are treated as if they were human beings, with human attributes and feelings

simile a figure of speech in which something is said to be 'like' or 'as' another thing

soliloquy (from the Latin 'to speak alone') dramatic convention which allows a character in a play to speak directly to the audience as if thinking aloud about motives, feelings and decisions

syntax the arrangement of words in a particular form and order so as to achieve meaning

Emma Smith is a Fellow in English Literature at Hertford College, Oxford. Her teaching and research interests are in the drama of Shakespeare and his contemporaries. She was born in Leeds and educated at Somerville College, Oxford.

Maya Angelou
I Know Why the Caged Bird Sings

Jane Austen
Pride and Prejudice

Alan Ayckbourn
Absent Friends

Elizabeth Barrett Browning
Selected Poems

Robert Bolt
A Man for All Seasons

Harold Brighouse
Hobson's Choice

Charlotte Brontë
Jane Eyre

Emily Brontë
Wuthering Heights

Shelagh Delaney
A Taste of Honey

Charles Dickens
David Copperfield
Great Expectations
Hard Times
Oliver Twist

Roddy Doyle
Paddy Clarke Ha Ha Ha

George Eliot
Silas Marner
The Mill on the Floss

Anne Frank
The Diary of a Young Girl

William Golding
Lord of the Flies

Oliver Goldsmith
She Stoops to Conquer

Willis Hall
The Long and the Short and the Tall

Thomas Hardy
Far from the Madding Crowd
The Mayor of Casterbridge
Tess of the d'Urbervilles
The Withered Arm and other Wessex Tales

L.P. Hartley
The Go-Between

Seamus Heaney
Selected Poems

Susan Hill
I'm the King of the Castle

Barry Hines
A Kestrel for a Knave

Louise Lawrence
Children of the Dust

Harper Lee
To Kill a Mockingbird

Laurie Lee
Cider with Rosie

Arthur Miller
The Crucible
A View from the Bridge

Robert O'Brien
Z for Zachariah

Frank O'Connor
My Oedipus Complex and Other Stories

George Orwell
Animal Farm

J.B. Priestley
An Inspector Calls
When We Are Married

Willy Russell
Educating Rita
Our Day Out

J.D. Salinger
The Catcher in the Rye

William Shakespeare
Henry IV Part I
Henry V
Julius Caesar
Macbeth
The Merchant of Venice
A Midsummer Night's Dream
Much Ado About Nothing

Romeo and Juliet
The Tempest
Twelfth Night

George Bernard Shaw
Pygmalion

Mary Shelley
Frankenstein

R.C. Sherriff
Journey's End

Rukshana Smith
Salt on the snow

John Steinbeck
Of Mice and Men

Robert Louis Stevenson
Dr Jekyll and Mr Hyde

Jonathan Swift
Gulliver's Travels

Robert Swindells
Daz 4 Zoe

Mildred D. Taylor
Roll of Thunder, Hear My Cry

Mark Twain
Huckleberry Finn

James Watson
Talking in Whispers

Edith Wharton
Ethan Frome

William Wordsworth
Selected Poems

A Choice of Poets

Mystery Stories of the Nineteenth Century including The Signalman

Nineteenth Century Short Stories

Poetry of the First World War

Six Women Poets

For the AQA Anthology:

Duffy and Armitage & Pre-1914 Poetry

Heaney and Clarke & Pre-1914 Poetry

Poems from Different Cultures

Margaret Atwood
Cat's Eye
The Handmaid's Tale

Jane Austen
Emma
Mansfield Park
Persuasion
Pride and Prejudice
Sense and Sensibility

Alan Bennett
Talking Heads

William Blake
Songs of Innocence and of
Experience

Charlotte Brontë
Jane Eyre
Villette

Emily Brontë
Wuthering Heights

Angela Carter
Nights at the Circus

Geoffrey Chaucer
The Franklin's Prologue and Tale
The Merchant's Prologue and
Tale
The Miller's Prologue and Tale
The Prologue to the Canterbury
Tales
The Wife of Bath's Prologue and
Tale

Samuel Coleridge
Selected Poems

Joseph Conrad
Heart of Darkness

Daniel Defoe
Moll Flanders

Charles Dickens
Bleak House
Great Expectations
Hard Times

Emily Dickinson
Selected Poems

John Donne
Selected Poems

Carol Ann Duffy
Selected Poems

George Eliot
Middlemarch
The Mill on the Floss

T.S. Eliot
Selected Poems
The Waste Land

F. Scott Fitzgerald
The Great Gatsby

E.M. Forster
A Passage to India

Brian Friel
Translations

Thomas Hardy
Jude the Obscure
The Mayor of Casterbridge
The Return of the Native
Selected Poems
Tess of the d'Urbervilles

Seamus Heaney
Selected Poems from 'Opened
Ground'

Nathaniel Hawthorne
The Scarlet Letter

Homer
The Iliad
The Odyssey

Aldous Huxley
Brave New World

Kazuo Ishiguro
The Remains of the Day

Ben Jonson
The Alchemist

James Joyce
Dubliners

John Keats
Selected Poems

Philip Larkin
The Whitsun Weddings and
Selected Poems

Christopher Marlowe
Doctor Faustus
Edward II

Arthur Miller
Death of a Salesman

John Milton
Paradise Lost Books I & II

Toni Morrison
Beloved

George Orwell
Nineteen Eighty-Four

Sylvia Plath
Selected Poems

Alexander Pope
Rape of the Lock & Selected
Poems

William Shakespeare
Antony and Cleopatra
As You Like It
Hamlet
Henry IV Part I
King Lear
Macbeth
Measure for Measure
The Merchant of Venice
A Midsummer Night's Dream
Much Ado About Nothing
Othello
Richard II
Richard III
Romeo and Juliet
The Taming of the Shrew
The Tempest
Twelfth Night
The Winter's Tale

George Bernard Shaw
Saint Joan

Mary Shelley
Frankenstein

Jonathan Swift
Gulliver's Travels and A Modest
Proposal

Alfred Tennyson
Selected Poems

Virgil
The Aeneid

Alice Walker
The Color Purple

Oscar Wilde
The Importance of Being
Earnest

Tennessee Williams
A Streetcar Named Desire
The Glass Menagerie

Jeanette Winterson
Oranges Are Not the Only
Fruit

John Webster
The Duchess of Malfi

Virginia Woolf
To the Lighthouse

William Wordsworth
The Prelude and Selected
Poems

W.B. Yeats
Selected Poems

Metaphysical Poets